Tuning In

LISA AIKEN

DEVORA
PUBLISHING
JERUSALEM ◆ NEW YORK

Tuning In
Published by DEVORA PUBLISHING COMPANY

Text Copyright © 2004 by Lisa Aiken
Cover and Book Design: Yael Kanner
Editor: Devora Talia Gordon

All rights reserved. No part of this book may be reproduced or transmitted in any or by any means, electronic or mechanical, including photocopying, recording, or by any information storage and retrieval system, without permission in writing from the publisher.

Library of Congress Cataloging-in-Publication Data

Aiken, Lisa.
Tuning in / Lisa Aiken.
p. cm.
ISBN 1-930143-92-3 (hardcover : alk. paper) – ISBN 1-932687-07-6 (pbk. : alk. paper)
1. Jewish way of life–Anecdotes. 2. Spiritual life–Judaism–Anecdotes. 3. Interpersonal relations–Religious aspects–Judaism–Anecdotes. 4. Life-
-Religious aspects–Judaism. I. Title.

BM723.A38 2004
296.7'2–dc22
2004004604
ISBN: 1-930143-92-3 (HC)
ISBN: 1-932687-07-6 (PB)

Email: sales@devorapublishing.com
Web Site: www.devorapublishing.com
Printed in Israel

Table of Contents

Foreword	7
Introduction	11
Part I: Finding Our Soul-Mate	***23***
A Whale of a Tale	25
In Sickness and In Health	31
Part II: Everyone is a Messenger	***37***
The Split Second	39
On a Wing and a Prayer	49
Brother, Can You Spare A…Friend?	55
Part III: Having Children	***65***
The Right Place at the Right Time	67
Nothing is Inconceivable for God	71
The Infinitesimal Chance	83
Part IV: What Goes Around, Comes Around	***99***
Reaping What We Sow	101
A War Story	115
Auschwitz and Antibiotics	117
Part V: Journeys of the Soul	***127***
It's Not Your Time Yet	129
From Here to Eternity	135
Part VI: Money Matters	***139***
Mary's Message	141
The Heavenly Accountant	151
All You Have To Do Is Ask	155
Part VII: Brushes with Mortality	***165***
The Verdict	167
Fireworks, Friends, and the Fourth of July	173
A Leap of Faith	181
What You Don't Know Can Heal You	189

*This book is dedicated to
Chaim Sarya ben Eliezer, of blessed memory.*

Acknowledgements

I would like to thank Devorah Talia Gordon for the extraordinary skill, patience, and dedication that she showed while editing this book. I would also like to express my appreciation to Yaacov Peterseil and Julie Waldman for the care and professionalism that they showed in publishing this book. It was a pleasure to work with all of them.

Foreword

Watching American plays, musicals, movies and television; listening to contemporary music; and reading popular newspapers, magazines, and bestsellers, one might think that Americans are anti-spiritual and non-religious. Yet, most Americans, not to mention people in the world at large, are religious. At least ninety percent of Americans believe in God, and a majority of them believe that He guides them in their daily lives. When the Industrial Revolution changed the world, some people replaced religion with science and technology. Instead of seeking comfort and meaning in spirituality and a Divine plan for the world, some people tried to immerse themselves in scientific and philosophical explanations of life that excluded a Divine power. Now that the world has become incredibly technologically advanced, people are questing for the spirituality that was temporarily supplanted by secularism. Since the latter part of the twentieth century, people have been feeling the lack of a personal, Divine being Who guides them and gives their lives direction and meaning. People feel the void of a personal God, who is both all-powerful yet loving, and they seek a deity who continually watches over them and responds to them and the world moment by moment.

Whether or not people have a religious belief system, there is an almost universal desire for people to receive signs that God exists and communicates with us. We want to know that a deity not only created the universe in which we live, but is involved in our day-to-day lives in a caring and loving way.

One barrier to believing in a deity who cares about the smallest details of our lives is that we don't hear Him communicating with us. If He doesn't communicate with us in a way that we recognize, or appreciate His input, we can easily stop trying to seek Him. No one wants a one-way relationship!

Judaism, which taught the world about one God, teaches that the Almighty created the world only so that we would have the pleasure of an eternal, loving relationship with Him. Anyone can earn that eternal relationship by acting in moral and Godly ways. We do this while we are alive and our souls reside in our bodies. The more we learn about, then act like God, the more we can put ourselves on a wavelength where we notice Him communicating with us.

If a person has a radio but never turns it on, he might conclude that radio waves don't exist, and that radios are silent boxes that do nothing. Once someone shows the radio's owner how to turn it on and tune into the right frequencies, he simultaneously opens up a rich world of communication that the listener never noticed existed before.

This book was written to help readers tune in to their spiritual frequencies. We all have "supernatural" experiences. We are all privy to Divine communication, but may not recognize it as such. In retrospect, we might realize that we dismissed messages that we received, forgot our experiences, or reduced them to insignificance. By allowing ourselves to hear the Divine Voice calling out to us in our daily lives, we can live with a higher level of consciousness. Instead of going through life spiritually unconscious, we can forge an ever-closer relationship with the One Who put us here. By appreciating how much He constantly tries to communicate with us, we can see our lives as a great mosaic pieced together by a loving Creator. As long as the picture is in process, we might not know how it will make a coherent whole someday. Yet, tuning in to the right frequencies now, and opening ourselves up to Divine providence, will make our journeys much more interesting and fulfilling.

Going on a long trip with no apparent destination is a very frustrating and often meaningless experience. Going on the same trip while knowing that our Heavenly Parent is holding our hand allows us to confront each obstacle and vista along a very different journey.

Some readers may be skeptical that they could receive Divine communication in their lives, or that others can receive it with regularity. All too often, we go through life finding only what we expect to find. If we would keep a daily log of our experiences, and start thinking about how they fit into a spiritual framework, we might be amazed at how frequently we receive Divine messages. If we ask those around us to tell us their stories, with an eye to their spiritual significance, we will find many fascinating books waiting to be read.

It is the author's hope that this book will encourage readers to hear the Divine Voice that frequently calls to us with messages of hope, love and inspiration. By tuning in to these higher frequencies, we need never feel disconnected from our Source.

The author made every effort to accurately report the incidents that occurred in this book. Nevertheless, in order to protect the anonymity of the people involved, almost all names and some identifying details have been changed. I am indebted to those who shared their stories with me, and hope they will inspire countless others the way they have inspired me.

Introduction

For many years, I wanted to write a book of stories but never did. Stories that people told me, and experiences that I had, simply sat in the recesses of my mind until my father, of blessed memory, passed away. I felt an outpouring of Divine providence before and after his funeral that compelled me to share my experiences, and my stories, with others. As listeners told me how moved they were by my words, I decided that I would record them in the present book.

My father, of blessed memory, was born on April 13, 1924, in Baltimore, Maryland. He passed away September 2, 2002, in Miami Beach, Florida. When I thought about who he was and how he lived his life, several episodes seemed especially remarkable.

My father grew up during the Depression and started earning a living while he was still a teenager. He went to work in his father's clothing manufacturing factory, known then as the *shmatta* business. Today, most clothing manufacturing takes place in third world countries where labor is very cheap. In the early 1900s, many Jewish businessmen ran such factories in the eastern United States.

When my grandfather, an immigrant from Vilna, Lithuania, started the Mayflower Manufacturing Company in Baltimore in the early 1900s, he was one of the first whites in the business to employ blacks. (They were called Negroes in those days.) When I was a child, my father employed about three hundred blacks in his factories. Nearly all of them were women, including the foreladies. He trained many of these women himself and paid them a good salary, neither of which would have happened without his concern that they have better lives.

It was not until I was an adult that I discovered that my father had been threatened on occasion with having blinding acid thrown in his face, and worse, for his daring behavior.

During the 1960s, there were race riots in Baltimore. Many stores in the downtown area were burned or were looted. The elevator operator in my father's factory was an elderly, frail, black man with light skin. He had short white curls on his head and his hands no longer worked as well as they once had. Earl put his thin, arthritic arm around my father, who at that point was far stronger and taller than Earl was, and promised, "Mr. Aiken, I'll make sure that no one touches your place." Despite the massive looting and burning that transpired soon after, my father's factories remained undisturbed.

In the midst of the civil rights movement, a troublemaker reported my father to the authorities for prejudice against blacks. An investigator, who knew nothing about my father, showed up unexpectedly at his office and accused my father of discrimination against blacks in his hiring practices.

"Just a minute," my father told him. "Let me speak to my forelady about this." With that, he hollered above the din of the factory full of sewing machines and called over Pauline. Pauline, as black as the ace of spades, waded past her one hundred and fifty black and two white charges to my father's desk. As the investigator's eyes bugged out, my father, in mock chiding tones, told her, "Pauline, if you ever hear that there is any discrimination going on here, you let me know immediately."

The investigator closed his briefcase and made a hasty exit, never to return.

The shmatta business had many downsides to it. For example, the manufacturers had to imagine what types of clothes would be fashionable a season in advance. It sometimes happened that the buyers for the retail stores in New York, the main market for the goods that manufacturers produced, would make orders. The buyers then changed their minds after the manufacturers had already started production. At other times, stores would order clothing, and then cancel contracts already being manufactured because a better offer came along. Although my father discussed almost nothing of his work life with his children, he did make one thing perfectly clear to me when I was old enough to understand. A person's word is his word. In business, you get a reputation from delivering on your promises. Even if he took a financial loss from following through on agreements that he made, he never followed the popular route of lying to protect his interests. Even when he realized that, due to an unanticipated hike in the price of raw materials, it would cost him more to make a line of clothing than he received for producing it, he provided what he had said he would. I understood, from the few conversations to which I was privy, that this living up to his word when others lacked integrity was not an infrequent occurrence.

By the time my father came home at the end of his eleven-hour day, his nerves were shot. The stress of working in the deafening noise of his factories, with constant production deadlines, and with buyers who sometimes changed their minds on a whim, took its toll. Nevertheless, my father took it upon himself to use his business skills after hours to help others.

When my older brother and sister attended the local Jewish elementary schools, both the Talmudical Academy and Bais Yaakov parochial schools in Baltimore were in danger of going bankrupt. My father intervened at night after he came home from work. There were many parents of Bais Yaakov girls who had enough money to buy cars, take vacations and send their children to summer camp, yet they cried poverty when the principal of the school asked them to pay their children's tuition. My father was outraged. He personally made telephone calls to parents and told them that if they didn't pay their bills, their children would have to go elsewhere for their education. Miraculously, the very parents who insisted that they couldn't afford the tuition settled their bills in full.

Then there was the matter of transportation. There were not enough children in those days to warrant hiring buses to transport the boys and girls separately to their respective schools. My father insisted that both boys and girls go on the same buses in order to reduce costs, something the school administrators wouldn't countenance.

"We can't have boys and girls going to school together," the principals asserted.

"Then you won't have any schools at all because they will go bankrupt," my father proclaimed, not backing down.

Thanks to my father's business acumen and adamancy, both the Talmudical Academy and Bais Yaakov in Baltimore are thriving institutions for Jewish children more than forty years later.

When my sister and I were in college, finding Jewish men to date became an important, and difficult, matter. My sister attended Goucher College, the sister school of Johns Hopkins University. At that time, Goucher was still an all-female school, and Hopkins was still largely male. The most likely place for my sister to find eligible men was at Hopkins, which allowed its students to take a few classes at Goucher, and vice versa. Unfortunately, there was no place for Jewish singles at either Goucher or at Hopkins to meet one another. There were no kosher dining facilities at either school, and the few Hopkins students who were resolute about keeping kosher lived in one or two apartments near the campus.

My father resolved to do something about this. For at least a year, I recall him sitting at his desk making countless phone calls to remedy the situation. All freshmen were required to join the regular university meal plan, whether they ate the food or not. My father resolutely maintained that Hopkins had to have a kosher dining hall, or KDH, as he affectionately referred to it.

"Give students a choice as to whether they want to join the regular meal plan or a kosher meal plan," he insisted to the administration. He knew that without a KDH there was virtually no way that Jewish students who lived in the dormitories could keep kosher. They had no opportunities to buy or cook kosher food.

My father was also very concerned about intermarriage, which was nowhere near the epidemic that it is today. Without a kosher dining facility, where were Jewish students going to find each other among the sea of non-Jews? Going to Israeli folk dancing or to sporadic Jewish events on campus were the only options. At least if there was a KDH, he reasoned, Jewish students could meet one another in a relaxed atmosphere that might eventually lead to marriage.

As he spent countless hours advising, cajoling, recommending, and listening, he encountered one barrier after another. One thing I learned from my father is that when something is important, one must have dogged determination. He certainly did. When the final barrier was thrown up – there was no funding for this project, without which it wouldn't get off the ground – my father donated his own money to make sure that his dreams would become a reality.

I still remember the concerned look on my father's face as he placed the call to the person who was in charge of the KDH that first year. "So how many students signed up for the kosher meal plan?" he inquired.

His critics had insisted that only a handful of students kept kosher, and there would not be enough interest in the KDH to make it viable. They were convinced that his plan would be too costly given the minuscule number of students who would participate.

As he listened to the response on the other end of the phone, a broad smile lit up his face. "Fifty students are eating there? That's fifty Jewish students who can now keep kosher, even though most of them didn't keep kosher before! And that's fifty Jewish singles who now have a chance to meet other Jews!" There was a pause as he listened intently, then chuckled. "And they say that the food there is better than in the regular cafeteria? That's the way it should be."

During the past thirty-plus years, I had no idea as to what had become of the KDH. During the years that we lived in Baltimore, I knew that hundreds of Jewish students had met and eaten kosher food because of my father's vision. Yet, such institutions often come and go, and it seemed likely that the KDH had as well.

As I was writing this book, a few months after my father's passing, an amazing encounter occurred. I had spoken about my father and the KDH in the eulogy that I gave at his funeral. I then wondered for days about what had happened to the institution that he had spent so much time and energy launching.

A few months later, I went to a bar mitzvah in Jerusalem where I encountered a rabbi who lived in Baltimore. As we chatted, he told me that he had heard about my father's passing and expressed his condolences on my loss. I soon discovered that he was a kosher supervisor in my hometown, and I asked him if he knew anything about the Johns Hopkins University kosher dining hall.

"Yes," he replied, "I know a lot about it. I am the *kashrut* (kosher) supervisor there!" The rabbi informed me that at the time we spoke, three hundred college students ate there on a regular basis.

Another event that happened during my teen years made an indelible impression on me. After working for many years as a clothing manufacturer, my father made a transition to producing disposable textiles. These included products such as throwaway tablecloths and disposable hospital clothing. In the days before rigorous laboratory testing, he used to test the flammability of nonwoven hospital gowns, operating room drapes, and tablecloths by throwing them in our living room fireplace and seeing if they burned! He was one of the pioneers in the field of these everyday products that we now take for granted.

After spending many nerve-racking years producing clothing, he got an offer of a lifetime. An international company bought his factories and hired him to work as their production manager during the first few years after their taking over. After the initial transition, the paper company had the option of offering him continued employment at a very generous salary.

My father was thrilled to have sold his factories. Most people in his line of work either continually plowed back into the business whatever profits they made, or they struggled to break even. By that time, the only way to recoup a lifelong investment in that business was to sell it. Many owners were not able to do that, at least not profitably. Eventually, clothing-manufacturing factories in the United States became dinosaurs as the markets were moved to the Far East and other third-world countries.

My father was very pleased to finally have a steady, predictable income for the first time in his life. After all, he had five children to take care of, and three of them would soon be in college. As often happens to us all, as soon as he became complacent with his life, the One Above sent challenges to spur him to grow spiritually.

My father was not raised in an observant Jewish home. Nevertheless, when he was in his early thirties, he began to study Judaism with a rabbi and decided to keep kosher. It was not until he was in his mid-forties, long after he had sold his factories, that he started observing the Sabbath and Jewish holidays in the traditional manner.

Before he became a Sabbath observer, our family celebrated many holiday traditions, such as attending synagogue and eating special meals on Passover and the Jewish New Year. Yet, my father did not observe the traditional restrictions of not driving a car, not working, or not speaking on the telephone on those days.

The company that bought his factories was very WASPy, and my father was the only Jewish executive that they had ever hired. My father did not want to make waves that might jeopardize his position, and he did his best to integrate quietly into the company. At the beginning of my father's tenure, a top executive in the company named Tom called to welcome him aboard.

"Sidney, we have an annual meeting of all of the top executives from the company in September. Since you are new here, and few of our people know you, we thought that it would be critical for you to join us for this. You will need to apprise our people of what you know in the field of disposable textile manufacturing. We went to great lengths to contact all of our executives who will be meeting in Philadelphia on September 18. We'll see you there."

People often think, mistakenly, that if someone is religious, he should have an easy life. Judaism teaches us that life is about continually confronting spiritual and moral challenges that spur us to grow. Successfully overcoming those challenges allows us to actualize our soul's potential that would otherwise remain dormant. So, as soon as someone takes steps to become more spiritually or morally committed, we can expect that God will send him or her challenges to test how strongly they will stay committed to their convictions.

A person who begins to eat only kosher (ritually fit) food can expect that there will soon be an invitation to attend a family wedding, bar mitzvah, or anniversary party where nonkosher food will be served. A single man or woman who resolves that marrying someone Jewish is important will meet the gentile of their dreams. A doctor who learns about Jewish medical ethics will be asked to perform a procedure that violates the religious codes, or will be confronted by a chance to procure a lot of money by engaging in unethical or illegal behavior. Every event of our lives is designed by the Master of the World to enable us to maximally develop our spiritual connection with Him, sometimes at the expense of our momentary pleasure or comfort.

So, as soon as my father and Tom ended their conversation, my father took out his schedule book. To his horror, he saw that September 18 was Rosh Ha'Shana, the Jewish New Year. He had gone to the synagogue on Rosh Ha'Shana every year for decades. How could he now attend an executive meeting in a Philadelphia hotel instead?

Before he picked up the phone to call Tom back, he called his Jewish associate manager to tell him the bad news. I don't know what Dan told my father, but I heard my father's side of the conversation.

"Yes, I know that we just got the contract, and if we make waves they will not renew it." Pause. My father listened intently.

"Yes, I know that they might even consider it a breach of the present contract if we don't show up at the meeting, and they might fire us."

Dan obviously continued voicing his concerns on the other end of the line.

"Yes," my father said evenly, "I know that we are both in our forties, and if we lose this job, the job market is not likely to afford us another one." Another pause. My father waited for the next objection.

My father reiterated, "Dan, I know that we both have families to support, and we are both afraid of making waves with this company since they hire us at their pleasure. But I also know that being Jewish is important, and we are not going to that meeting on Rosh Ha'Shana." A few moments later, my father wordlessly put down the phone.

My father sat pensively at his desk, staring through the floor-to-ceiling den windows to the hedges on the far side of the porch. I could tell that he was weighing many considerations deliberately and simultaneously before he picked up the telephone receiver again.

His lips were pursed and his jaw was set with determination, while his face looked strained. He dialed a ten-digit number. I sensed from the heaviness in the air that he felt like a prisoner who was about to hear a terrible sentence from the court. A few moments later, the secretary put his call through to the vice president of the company.

"Tom, this is Sid Aiken. I have to talk to you about something very important. I know that you went to incredible lengths to arrange the executive meeting so that I could be there."

Tom interrupted, "You bet I did. It took me days to coordinate everyone's schedule because we have our top people coming in from around the country to meet you."

My father hesitated, but didn't get derailed. "I'm sorry, Tom, but I have some bad news for you. You see, there is one day in the entire year that is holier to Jews than any other day, and that day is called Rosh Ha'Shana. The day that you scheduled the meeting is Rosh Ha'Shana, the Jewish New Year. I'm afraid that neither Dan nor I can come to a business meeting that day. We need to be in the synagogue instead."

I can only imagine the hushed silence that must have confronted my father at that moment. I gathered that Tom ended the conversation by saying something to the effect that my father's refusal to attend the meeting would not be taken lightly.

I'm sure that as disturbed as my father had been by Tom's reaction, Dan was even less pleased. He was inclined to attend the meeting, but my father was adamant that neither of them would go. Since my father had been instrumental in helping Dan get his job with the new company, Dan was not willing to go without him.

A week later, Tom called again. "Sidney, I want you to know that I went to considerable lengths to reschedule our executive meeting because of you. I decided that we couldn't have the meeting without you. After spending hours on the phone, we found one last date that everyone could come to Philadelphia. We've rescheduled the meeting for September 27."

My father's heart sank. He perfunctorily checked his calendar, but he didn't need to do so. He already knew that September 27 was Yom Kippur, the Jewish Day of Atonement. Jews around the world fast for twenty-five hours on that day, and spend most of that time praying in the synagogue and repenting.

My father responded almost immediately, although I'm sure that he had never anticipated that he would be in such a terrible position with his new employer.

"Tom, thank you for your consideration and the enormous time and thought that you put into rescheduling the meeting for me. Unfortunately, there is only day of the year that is more holy than Rosh Ha'Shana, and that day is Yom Kippur. The day that you rescheduled the meeting is Yom Kippur. I'm sorry, but neither Dan nor I can attend."

Listening to the conversation, I can only imagine what my father must have felt at that moment. I gathered by my father's series of "I know that you need me there," and "I'm sorry, but I can't come on that day," that Tom did not back down graciously. It was clear that he also implied that my father's unwillingness to "get dispensation" or "bend the rules" might cost my father his job. My father stood his ground.

And so, that year my father and Dan spent the High Holidays in their respective synagogues. When the newspaper came the morning after Yom Kippur, my father perused the stock market pages. He rarely looked at that part of the newspaper because he never invested in stocks. Yet that morning, he had a grin on his face that I never understood for many years.

He proudly told a relative in my presence, years later, that the stock price of the paper company that had bought him out had reached an all-time high that Yom Kippur. My father took it as a Divine wink that validated his belief that one never loses by doing the right thing.

My father wanted to be known as a good businessman, and that he was. While he was interested in Jewish education, and he took great delight in attending my lectures the few times that he could attend, his formal Jewish education was not impressive. However, what he did as a Jewish businessman was extraordinary. Through his kindness, concern, and willingness to make new things happen that never occurred before, he touched the lives of thousands.

When a person's soul goes to the next world, it is asked a few questions. The first is, "Did you give and take honestly in business?" I believe that when my father's soul met its Maker, he took some impressive accounting sheets with him. May this eulogy encourage others to follow in his footsteps by using their skills and talents to make the world a better place, especially when it takes self-sacrifice to do so.

Part 1:
Finding Our Soul-Mate

A Whale of a Tale

Ruth was a cheerful, twenty-five-year-old secretary at SeaWorld of Ohio. Her department did landscaping, filtration and maintenance for the park. SeaWorld was a very interesting place during the summer when its attractions were open, but things were much slower when they closed for the winter. Every March or April, animals were brought to Ohio from SeaWorld in San Diego, and they were returned to California every September. When the animals were away, a skeleton staff worked in the office, and workmen did repairs and maintained the pools of water to ensure that the park would be ready to open in the spring.

One summer, Ruth had lost her usual cheerfulness and was reeling from the breakup of a serious relationship. She came to work one morning and confided to a co-worker named Roger how devastated she was by the separation from her boyfriend. Meanwhile, as tears flowed down her face, a man walked over. In the midst of her sadness, Roger introduced her to a man he called Pete. Ruth was in another world and paid little attention to the stranger.

A few weeks later, Ruth sat under a leafy willow tree outside her house one night. The coolness of the evening sent an initial chill through her body. She peered up at the stunning night sky, and noticed the brightness of the moonlight and the billions of stars spilled across the heavens. She marveled at the Creator's awesome power and abilities. She had no doubt that He could do anything. Perhaps He would even help her get over her loss. She pleaded with Him, "Please send me someone to love."

Tuning In

By now it was Labor Day weekend, and the park was readying to close. The veterinarian of SeaWorld, Doc, was coordinating the moving of all of the animals back to San Diego via the airport. He asked Ruth if she would be willing to work the day of "The Move," which was not a usual workday. Ruth agreed. Doc told the staff to meet at the cafeteria that morning at 3:00 A.M. and have breakfast before starting their day's work.

When Ruth stepped out of her house that morning, she had anticipated that the air would be freezing. She was right. As her breath frosted, she was glad that she had bundled herself to the hilt. She was barely visible under her dull green army jacket, two pairs of black pants, a bulky brown hat, scarf, and gloves. She got into her car under the cover of darkness and drove in the still of the night to SeaWorld.

When she arrived, she joined the rest of the workers in the cafeteria. After the staff ate oatmeal, pancakes and eggs, then drank some steaming coffee to keep them warm and awake, Doc assigned everyone to work at a different area – the whale stadium, the seal and otter stadium, and so on. Ruth was assigned to the whale stadium.

"Okay," Doc exhorted, "let's get to work."

Ruth got up, dumped her breakfast leftovers into the garbage bin, and put away her tray. When she turned around, she noticed a tall, blond man standing next to her.

"I heard Doc call your name to work in the whale stadium," he told her. "I'm working there, too. Do you mind if I walk over there with you?"

"No," Ruth replied.

The two of them spent the next ten minutes talking on the way to the stadium. "By the way, you can call me Smithie," the stranger told Ruth.

All the while, it never dawned on Ruth that this man with whom she was speaking was the same one that she had met one week earlier, whom Roger had introduced as "Pete." She found it very peculiar that this trainer called himself Smithie. After all, she had spent the summer

Finding Our Soul-Mate

talking to an animal trainer who called himself Smithie, who bore little resemblance to this man.

"Who do you think you're kidding?" she thought to herself. "Do you want me to believe that there are two animal trainers here named Smithie?"

(As it turned out, the Smithie to whom she had spoken all summer had been pulling a prank. He was indeed a whale trainer, but his real name was not Smithie.)

By this time, the real Smithie and Ruth had reached the whale stadium. Smithie had a touch of disappointment in his voice as he announced, "Well, I've got to go catch a whale." With that, he disappeared into the cavernous building.

Ruth didn't know it at the time, but the Smithie that she had just met was a great whale trainer. He had a special relationship with Kona, known to the rest of the world as Shamu. Kona had cataracts and was initially thought unable to be trained, but Smithie had a way with her. She became one of SeaWorld's star performers, and she and Smithie became very attached to one another. She even loved for him to pet her. He became a celebrity working with whales and delighted the audience when he appeared on television.

After Smithie disappeared, Ruth and the other staff waited outside in the freezing cold for him to catch his whale. As uncomfortable as it was outdoors, it was not much more hospitable in the whale tank, where the water temperature was in the high 40's.

For those of you who have never tried it, catching a whale is not so easy. The trick is for the trainer to try to convince the whale to swim into a sling that has been lowered by a crane into the whale tank. If the whale obliges, it centers itself on the sling in a way that the trainer can slip the pectoral fins into the huge holes cut into the sling. Then, when the enormous animal is centered, the crane lifts it up and places it into a flatbed truck for transport to the airport. The whale needn't be kept under water during transport, but its skin had to be kept moist or it would dry out and crack. At least, this is how it was done nearly thirty years ago. It was Ruth's job to keep the animal covered with lanolin.

Tuning In

Unfortunately for Smithie, Kona wasn't cooperating. She had a mind of her own, and that morning it didn't include being scooped up in a sling. Finally, having no alternative, Smithie, in his wet suit, jumped into the pool. The cold water was almost heart-stopping, even in a wet suit. Using all of his trainer wits, he did his best to coax the massive mammal into the sling. It wasn't easy. Hours later, she finally centered herself so that she could be moved.

In what seemed to take an eternity, the whale was finally loaded onto the truck, and people from all over town came to wish goodbye to Shamu and the rest of her entourage until the next season.

When Ruth got to the airport, she saw an enormous Flying Tigers jet, waiting for the marine cargo. Doc came over to her and instructed, "Here, Ruth, is a big tub of lanolin. Your job is to cover the whale with lanolin everywhere that it needs, especially around the pectoral and dorsal fins." Ruth got down on her knees and began smearing the enormous black whale with emollient. She soon sensed someone standing there. She looked up and saw Smithie.

As Ruth rose to her feet, Smithie told her, "Look, I heard that you're going through a really tough time, and it must be so hard for you. I just want you to know – and I know that you don't even know me – but I want you to know that I care."

Ruth was so touched that she kissed him instinctively on the cheek, then recoiled in shock. She looked around to see if anyone had seen what she had done.

Before she could collect herself, Smithie had walked over to Shamu, and the lift was starting to elevate both of them into the jet. Smithie grabbed onto the frame surrounding the whale, and with the other hand, he waved goodbye to Ruth.

As the jet door closed, Ruth was overwhelmed with feelings for this stranger. She didn't understand what was happening to her. How could she have feelings for this man that she didn't even know? She asked God for clarity. Was she going crazy? She had only known this man for about fifteen minutes, and much of that time she had not been favorably impressed!

Finding Our Soul-Mate

When Ruth went home, she found herself unable to stop thinking about Smithie. She couldn't remember what he looked like, so the next day at work, she went to the public relations department. "Do you have any pictures of the animal trainers who worked here this summer?" she asked shyly.

In a few moments, they gave her a slew of photographs of Smithie training the whales that entire summer. "Wow, he's really cute!" she exclaimed. She had been so mournful the entire summer that she hadn't noticed how handsome Smithie was. He was in great shape, too.

Ruth decided to write him a note in care of the training department at SeaWorld in San Diego. She simply addressed it to Smithie, since she didn't even know his last name. She wrote, "Dear Smithie, Thank you for your kind words. They made me feel better. Ruth." She lost no time in mailing the letter. Normally, it took a letter three days to get to San Diego from Ohio.

The next day, Ruth got a letter at work, addressed to Ruth (with no last name), in care of the maintenance department at SeaWorld of Ohio. His note said, "It was really nice to meet you. I hope that your situation has improved. Smithie."

Every day after that, for the next two weeks, she wrote him a letter, and he wrote her a letter, and their letters continually crossed in the mail. She kept asking him questions, and before he could get her letter, she got a letter from him addressing those same questions!

The same happened from him to her.

In the meantime, Ruth was questioning her sanity. Was she just on the rebound? Could this man really care about her? At a friend's insistence, she finally called him to see what his intentions were. That resulted in Ma Bell making an absolute fortune during the next month. They made daily phone calls to each other that lasted for hours.

Before long, she visited him in California and they had a chance to get to know each other face-to-face. When it was time for her to go back to Ohio, it was clear that she would need to move to California if the relationship were to have a real chance at continuing.

Tuning In

In order to move to San Diego, Ruth needed to sell her house and furnishings. It was the beginning of the winter, and sales prospects for homes were not good. Once again, Ruth sat out under the willow tree in her yard and prayed. "Please God, help me sell my things so that I can move out to California." She then proceeded to make up a sign, "Everything I Own For Sale," and placed it at the end of her street.

Miraculously, people started showing up in droves, and by the end of the week everything she owned was sold. Within a month, she had closed on her house and was on a plane to San Diego. Two months later, Ruth and Smithie felt that their destiny was sealed. In their eyes, God had made a "done deal" with them, and they were married two months later.

Best of all, they are still happily married, more than two decades later.

In Sickness and In Health

Laurie was a sweet, appealing young woman, with golden brown, straight hair that fell to her shoulders. Her gray eyes were very expressive when she spoke, and she conveyed warmth and sincerity. After she graduated from high school, she got a job as a secretary. She had grown up in a Boston community where young women got married within a few years of graduation, yet that didn't happen to her. Several years after leaving school, no prospects of marriage were in the offing. She had dated here and there, but had not met anyone who was a serious candidate for marriage.

One day, she met Steve, a young man who was trying to start a business. Steve was ambitious, garrulous, enthusiastic and friendly. They were able to converse easily, and he made a nice impression on her. Later that week, he asked her out.

Laurie and Steve became serious about each over the next few months. She was sure that he would eventually propose to her, but he never did. The months stretched into years, until Laurie was twenty-four years old. She loved Steve, but he had a million excuses as to why he wasn't quite ready to make a commitment to marriage. At first, he insisted that he wasn't making enough money to support a family. Laurie waited patiently while Steve went from one job to another. He didn't last long at any of them.

Tuning In

And so it went for another year until Steve decided to go back to school. Meanwhile, Laurie watched as one after another of her friends got married. She finally gave Steve an ultimatum and he agreed to get engaged – privately. Laurie finally realized that only a therapist could cure his cold feet and she broke off their relationship.

Laurie found getting back into the dating scene overwhelming. She was neither a professional, nor drop-dead gorgeous, nor well-off financially, and she didn't want to compete for husbands with the many women who were. There were singles' events most weekends, usually involving hundreds of unattached women, and only half as many men. Laurie, being soft-spoken and shy, typically found herself talking to some nice women during those long evenings, but found very few men with whom there was mutual interest.

There were times when she met nice single men in more casual surroundings, but many of them tended to become friends with women. These couples had platonic relationships for years, but never ended up getting married. Laurie wanted to make sure that she didn't fall into that trap.

As the years went by, it was hard to maintain her optimism. Time and again, she recognized the same faces at singles' events. There was Lee, the thirty-two-year-old divorced computer programmer. He was looking for a woman who had not yet been born. Next to him was Tommy, the social work student who was too quiet for her taste. Chatting across from her was Manny. His ego was so enormous that it was surprising that there was room enough for anyone else in the building at the same time. Scott was at the far end. Ladies' gossip insisted that he was so indecisive that he would never get married, but he never missed an event. Laurie wondered as she went home at the end of the evening if any new men would come into the picture in the foreseeable future.

As weeks and months passed, Laurie began to wonder what went wrong. Why was it so difficult to find an attractive man with a good heart who had a sense of responsibility to others? She tried to avoid being like so many single women who lamented the lack of men who

Finding Our Soul-Mate

were good marriage material. While she tried to stay cheerful and avoid listening to friends' "war stories," she couldn't escape the fact that she and her friends were approaching and passing thirty. It was hard not to feel obsessed with the quest for a husband when everyone's anxiety about not getting married was thick enough to cut with a knife.

Laurie spent another two years going to events where she thought she might meet her soul-mate. Before each one she would wonder if the women would vastly outnumber the men, as typically happened. Would the same old crowd be there, or would there be new faces? It was so frustrating seeing the same people over and over again. Occasionally, she wondered if maybe, somehow, it could work between her and Jonathan. No, she thought, they had known each other for two years and there simply was no chemistry between them. Maybe she and Tommy should go out together? She vetoed that and continued down her list. She couldn't imagine going out with Fred, either. They simply didn't have enough common interests. Maybe Scott was mellowing with age, and he would be able to commit if she were the right woman. Her rational side called out, "Been there, done that. Do you want to waste another two years of your life?"

Laurie decided not to defer living now in the hope that she would get married some day. She attended weekly classes and socialized with her friends. She joined a group of students that played volleyball every week. She heard about a group of people who visited patients every Saturday at a local hospital and decided to join them as well. After all, it was so easy to become self-centered when one is single. She wanted to make sure that she had an opportunity to give to, and take care of, others while she was living alone.

The Saturday after she enrolled to visit patients, she and a handful of volunteers met at a central location and walked a few blocks to the hospital. When they arrived, the coordinator split them into pairs, each of which was assigned to visit three patients during the next hour and a half. She was paired with Tommy. They had seen each other many times over the years but their conversations had always been short and

Tuning In

superficial. Since neither had ever visited strangers in a hospital it was comforting at least to go with someone who wasn't a total stranger.

They entered the room of the first patient, Mr. Schloss. Laurie was not quite sure where to begin and was glad that Tommy began the conversation. Mr. Schloss was happy to have visitors, and soon spoke about the intense job and pressured life that contributed to the heart attack from which he was recovering. Laurie soon joined in and took turns with Tommy speaking and listening to Mr. Schloss. Before they knew it, the half-hour was up.

They went to Room 334 in the surgical wing, and found Lenny Green recovering from gallbladder surgery. By now, Laurie was feeling more comfortable talking to these strangers. She and Tommy made a great team cheering up the sixty-four-year-old man in the bleak hospital room.

Finally, their last visit of the day was to Sadie Stern. Sadie was an eighty-four-year-old great-grandmother who was recovering from a heart operation. When Tommy and Laurie entered her room, Sadie's eyes lit up. She had already been in the hospital for more than a week, so she knew what to expect from her visitors.

"I'm so glad to see you," she announced cheerfully. "Please come in."

Laurie and Tommy pulled up chairs next to her bed, and the three of them proceeded to chat about Sadie's life.

"I was beginning to feel a little depressed because I didn't have any other visitors today. Your visiting people like myself is so wonderful, you don't know.

"When my husband was alive, may he rest in peace, he would stay by my side and keep me company when I didn't feel well. I've had heart problems for quite a few years, and he was such a wonderful companion. He's been gone for seven years, and I still miss him. During the years that he worked, not a day went by that he didn't call me from the office and ask how I was. One day – we must have been married for about ten years – he told me that he needed to go away on business for three days. I helped him pack his suitcase, and it felt

Finding Our Soul-Mate

a little sad for both of us. We had never spent a night apart the entire time that we had been married. We said goodbye to each other the morning that he left, and he didn't call me that afternoon. It felt so strange. That evening, just as I was about to put dinner on the table for the children, my doorbell rang. I couldn't believe my eyes! It was Seymour.

"'What are you doing here?' I asked him.

"Do you know what he told me? He said, 'I love you so much I couldn't bear to be away from you.'

"We had such a great marriage. We were partners in every sense of the word. I couldn't have asked for a better husband. We did everything together once he retired. We loved to travel, but it didn't really matter where we were. We just loved to be in each other's company.

"Since he passed away, I keep myself busy with my grandchildren and with my great-grandchild. They're such blessings. Still, I miss my husband when I'm not distracted. It's not the same without him."

Tommy and Laurie sat wordlessly. Laurie took Sadie's hand and held it while a tear spilled silently onto Sadie's cheek.

"It's times like this when I miss Seymour the most. It's hard being old and not being in good health. I feel so vulnerable. When you have a good partner, you feel like you'll get through everything. When you're on your own, life's challenges feel much more difficult."

After a few moments Sadie gave Laurie's hand a squeeze. "So, are the two of you married?" Sadie asked.

Laurie and Tommy looked nervously at one another. "No," they both blurted out at the same time, and then broke into giggles.

"You should be," Sadie advised. "There's nothing as good as a good marriage."

The three of them chatted for a while longer until it was time for Laurie and Tommy to leave. As the pair walked down the long corridor, they felt as if they now knew each other in a much deeper way than they had before. They shared their reactions to Sadie with one another, and realized that they both wanted the same thing out of life: the kind of marriage that Sadie had had with Seymour.

Tuning In

"Laurie," Tommy asked nonchalantly, "do you have plans for tonight?"

Laurie knew as well as Tommy did that it wasn't "cool" not to have plans on a Saturday night. She didn't care. "No," she admitted, "I don't."

"Well," Tommy suggested, "could I ask you out for dinner? I'd love to continue this conversation with you."

"I'd love to," Laurie smiled.

They walked out of the hospital lobby into the pitch-black night. Laurie had found the attractive man with a good heart and a sense of responsibility to others that she had been seeking for many years. A few months later they were married.

Part II:
Everyone is a Messenger

The Split Second

When doing psychotherapy, therapists find that some patients are much easier to work with than others. Since the success of most psychotherapy depends upon the relationship that a therapist and patient have with each other, therapists select those patients with whom they can work well, and who will benefit from what that therapist has to offer. Therapists learn with experience not to take certain patients whose expectations or needs far exceed what the therapist can provide. To do otherwise frustrates the patient and overwhelms the therapist.

My "radar screen" went up the day that April came to see me for the first time. She spoke very intently as she told me about her life. She was the middle of three children. She had grown up in the suburbs of New York City, with an older brother who was hyperactive and a younger sister who was mildly retarded. April's mother was unable to spread her attention and devotion between three children, and April often got lost in the shuffle. Her father was a workaholic who loved his children from a distance, but whose idea of embracing a child was usually limited to holding a child while they posed for family pictures.

April understood, from a very early age, that it would not be wise for her to have many emotional needs. She did her best to take care of herself and not make waves. Her mother loved her for being a "good" girl who was easy to take care of, and who never seemed to have any problems that required the mother's extremely limited time.

By the time April was in high school, she suffered from chronic depression. She also had a very ominous family history. Her

Tuning In

grandfather had committed suicide, all three of her uncles suffered from depression, and her mother had suffered from postpartum depression after having her brother and sister. On the positive side, April was a bright young woman who did well in her classes. On the negative side, she often felt unhappy and did not get much nurturing from people in her life. She found it difficult to form close friendships because the emotional needs that she hid so well from her mother often surfaced with her peers.

She was very fortunate to have met a boy in her tenth-grade class who gave her the attention and caring that she craved. He seemed sincerely to have loved her, but she was never able to feel chemistry with him. By the end of high school, it became clear that they would part ways upon graduation. The prospect of facing life in a college where she had no friends would have overwhelmed her but for one saving grace. April was an excellent swimmer and joined the swim team. At least she had some social contact with others her age every morning before classes. She made friends with two other swimmers and felt successful as an athlete, regardless of whatever else was going on in her life.

Still, April struggled even then to get up many mornings. Luckily, having to be in the pool by 6:00 A.M. was a good motivator to get her out of bed every day. Despite her depression, she was a good student, and she graduated with a B-plus average. She completed a graduate course in accounting and went to work for an actuarial firm.

When April came to therapy, she was floundering at work and had no close relationships with men. Her family did not get along well with her. Her parents were not capable of understanding her and treated her more like a distant friend than as a daughter. April felt that she had little to which she could look forward, and never developed the coping mechanisms to deal with the normal disappointments of life.

Although she was twenty-six years old, she looked as if she were still in her teens. She had a pixie-like build, with mousy brown hair cut in layers, and freckles that dotted her cheeks and nose. She stared intently with her deep set, hazel eyes, and occasionally tossed her head in a way that made her long, dangling earrings clang softly. She usually wore nicely tailored dark pants and a simple pastel top, with casual shoes, and no makeup. While she did not spend much time grooming herself, at least she was not so depressed that she neglected how she looked.

As April recounted her background and the problems that brought her to seek help from me, every fiber in my body warned me not to take her as a patient. My time was already maximally committed and I could not afford to give her the time and attention that she was likely to need. The constellation of her symptoms made her a good candidate for attempting suicide in the future.

On the other hand, she had many strengths. She was intelligent, likeable, insightful, and a hard worker. She did not give up easily when faced with daunting challenges. She had used some mild recreational drugs in the past and had given them up. She did not drink alcohol, so at least I wouldn't have to worry about her complicating her problems by using drugs. She was also willing to see a psychiatrist and take antidepressant medication.

Still, a nagging voice inside told me that she was a ticking time bomb. She did not have good support systems. I fully expected that when she would feel overwhelmed, she would depend on me – probably for more than I could give her. At some point, I could imagine feeling completely drained, having exhausted whatever resources I could offer her. I worried about what April might do if she felt desperate.

"Dr. Aiken, I've interviewed a few other therapists over the past month, and I feel the best chemistry with you," she said optimistically. "I like your style, and I feel that you could help me. I didn't feel that about the other therapists that I consulted. Would you take me as your patient?"

I hesitated, thinking about how to word my rejection in the most palatable way possible. I would not be able to spend hours every day supporting a patient who would fall into a depressive abyss. She seemed likely to be just such a person.

Tuning In

"I'm sorry, April," I responded as diplomatically as I could, "I really don't have enough free hours to give you the time that you need and deserve." I couldn't even think of any colleagues to whom I could refer her. No one I knew had enough free time to give her what she might need.

Unwilling to give me an easy out, April was not easily deterred. "Dr. Aiken," she continued, "how many hours a week do you think that I need to be seen? I'm willing to make appointments with you at your convenience and to see you twice a week, if need be. I really believe that you can help me."

We went back and forth a few more times until April had convinced me that she would not be calling me in the middle of the night. She reassured me that she would deal with any crises she had in sessions instead of calling me outside of office hours, and she would honor my rules and boundaries.

"Fine," I relented, against my better judgment, "I will see you every week at 5:00 P.M. on Mondays and Thursdays." April grinned at my acceptance of her, while an ominous feeling stirred in the pit of my stomach.

April was a very determined patient. She always came to sessions on time; she was always prepared to talk about herself, her feelings, and her problems. She even kept a diary and took notes about what she needed to work on. She welcomed getting assignments about how to think and react more positively. At least for the first two months, working with April was very gratifying for us both.

Then it happened. April walked into my office one night after being verbally assaulted by her brother earlier that day. She described feeling as if the wind had been knocked out of her. Within minutes, she felt as if a Mack truck carrying a payload of depression had run her over and dumped its contents on her. After talking about her feelings for the rest of the session, I did not get the sense that we had made any headway. I recommended that she discuss her psychological deterioration with her psychiatrist and see if a change in her medication might help. She left our session feeling a bit more hopeful, but that feeling did not last.

Despite increasing our sessions to three times a week, and her following the psychiatrist's recommendations, her severe depression never lifted. In fact, it stayed remarkably stable with no end in sight. By the end of that month, she was put on notice at work that she had to take actuarial exams in a few months' time, and her continued employment was subject to her passing the tests. April was convinced that she would not be able to prepare adequately for the exams. She sank into a world of darkness from which neither she, nor I, nor her psychiatrist, could extricate her.

For those who have never been severely depressed, William Styron's very graphic description of how it feels can give them an almost palpable sense. One feels as if he has sunk into emotional quicksand and will never emerge feeling alive. The horror of it cannot be imagined by someone who has never had such an experience.

"Dr. Aiken," April reported listlessly one Monday afternoon, "I know that I won't do well on the exams. I can't concentrate and I can't memorize all of the material that I need to know. I feel that my brain is mired in molasses. I asked Dr. Myers if he can increase my meds, and he told me that there is nothing more that he can do for me. I think he's even getting fed up talking to me." She sat with her legs folded under her on my office couch. She had an expression on her face that was the picture of hopelessness. There is a look that patients have when they still expect that a remedy exists somewhere. That was totally absent from April's face. I could not detect the faintest glimmer of hope.

"Are you feeling suicidal?" I finally asked.

"I don't want to live like this, but I'm not suicidal. I can't imagine killing myself," she replied.

"If you ever feel that you are going to kill yourself, you must call me at once. If you can't reach me, call your psychiatrist. If you can't reach him, come to my hospital's emergency room. Are you willing to do that?" I inquired.

Tuning In

April nodded. "I really don't want to kill myself," she reassured me. The only problem was, I wasn't reassured.

It wasn't long before I felt as hopeless about April's getting better as she did. I had consulted numerous times with her psychiatrist and he confirmed what April had told me. He had given her every medication that might work and nothing was helping. He was also fed up with her desperate phone calls every day, and with her frantic cries for help framed by her hopelessness. My professional radar told me that April was at great risk of killing herself.

She was soon speaking to me every day by telephone, needing me to coax her through the day. My reassurances that every one of her depressions had eventually lifted fell on deaf ears. This time, she insisted, was worse than anything she had ever previously endured. She got no pleasure from any part of her life now. She had two friends, neither of whom wanted to be with her every day because she was such a black hole of doom and gloom. Her family was more of a problem than a solution. Her actuarial exams were looming and she did not know the material. Her boss was not pleased with her work. She did not want to go on living.

We now faced a Catch-22. Her psychiatrist was not willing to hospitalize April. If she were to admit that she felt like killing herself, any emergency room doctor could admit her to a psychiatric unit. However, she did not see any point in getting hospitalized. The psychiatrist had already told her that he would do nothing differently if she were in the hospital. By the time she would get out, her life would be unchanged except for the stigma of having had a psychiatric hospitalization. Even if I insisted that she go to an emergency room, she would simply tell the doctors there that she was not suicidal, and they would send her home. At best, she could be hospitalized against her will for forty-eight hours. At that point, she would simply say that she was feeling better and they would discharge her. I, like April, felt utterly helpless.

Several weeks passed, and April had gotten an extension on the date she needed to take her exams. She would be taking them several months later instead. I heaved a sigh of relief, thinking that this would take some pressure off of her. Still, even though she was speaking to me every day by telephone, and seeing me three times a week, she lived in an unrelenting black cloud that prevented her from feeling anything positive. The best that I could do was to figuratively hold her hand while she endured days and nights of feeling that she wanted to die.

One Friday morning, she called me bright and early. One symptom of her depression was waking up by 4:00 o'clock every day, only to spend the predawn hours dreading the day ahead. At 7:00, my phone rang, and we spent the next twenty minutes planning how she would make it through the weekend. Fortunately, a friend of hers was having a party Friday night. She had errands to run on Saturday, and Sunday a college friend would be in town. "Great," I thought to myself, "she has a reason to get out of bed every morning, and something to look forward to every day." It seemed reasonable to assume that she would be okay until she went back to work on Monday.

Friday afternoon, I packed a suitcase and my husband and I went to a friend's house for the Sabbath. I relished it more than usual, savoring the release from responsibility for someone else's life. In fact, by Saturday morning I had actually managed to forget about how shackled to April I had been feeling for weeks. My emotional batteries had been so drained that I felt like a sponge among cheerful people, soaking up every moment of good-humored banter, and relaxing at lunch with people who didn't speak about problems. I even managed to read a chapter in an interesting book that afternoon. By the time the Sabbath ended, I felt relaxed and refreshed.

When I got home around midnight, I was exhausted, and planned to go to bed as soon as possible. As I walked through the living room, I noticed the red light flashing on my answering machine. "Oh," I thought, "it's too late to call anyone back, but I may as well retrieve my messages now for tomorrow." I pressed the "play" button, and the machine dutifully recalled a message from 10:34 that evening:

Tuning In

"Hi, Dr. Aiken, it's April. I tried to call you and you weren't home. I can't take it any more. It's not your fault. You did what you could, and I thank you for it. I know that you tried to help me as best you could, but my life has been unbearable for so long. I don't want to go on living like this. Thanks for all of your help."

As the loud drone of the beep blared in the room that otherwise echoed silence, I felt a wave of panic take over my body. I glanced at my watch. It was 12:05. She had called one-and-a-half hours ago. A lot could have happened in that time. There was no time to waste. I took a deep breath as I dialed her number by rote. The phone rang. One ring. I counted the seconds. A second ring. More seconds. A third ring. "Please, God," I whispered, "don't let her be dead." I thought of two of my colleagues who had committed suicide in the prior two years, and the four patients of other colleagues who had killed themselves during that same time. I shuddered.

"Come on, April," I screamed inside my head, "answer the phone!" A fourth ring, followed by what seemed to be an endless silence. A fifth ring.

I thought about a friend's girlfriend. He had called her and found that her phone line was busy one afternoon, despite the fact that her telephone had call waiting. He ran to his car and drove like a fiend to her apartment, calling an ambulance in the meantime. He had a key to her apartment, and opened the door without knocking. He frantically raced through the living room into the bedroom and found her slumped over the bed, the bottle of sleeping pills inches away from her limp hand. By the time he got there, she was dead.

As the sixth ring echoed, I recalled April's address from my memory banks. I would have to call 911 as soon as I hung up. April lived in a studio apartment on a high floor. As the seventh ring resounded, I calculated that there was no way that it could take her more than five rings to pick up the phone if she were home and conscious. I would give it ten more seconds, I decided, as the eighth ring went unanswered. The ninth ring sent a piercing pain coursing through my gut, as I realized that the worst had probably already occurred. As I resigned myself to putting down the receiver, someone picked up the phone on the other end.

"Hello?" a surprised voice responded.

"Hi," I replied, wary of who might be answering the phone. "April?"

"Yes…Dr. Aiken?"

"Yes, April, it's me." Her tone of voice told me that she wasn't drugged, and that she had apparently not been in as much danger as I had feared. I heaved a sigh of relief. "I just heard your message and I was very worried about you. Are you okay?"

"Yes, I am…well, sort of. You see, the reason it took so long for me to pick up the phone is that after I called you and got your answering machine tonight, I decided to kill myself. I went out to the drugstore and bought myself a package of razor blades. I came back here and ran myself a warm bath and set the blades on the side of the tub. I had just gotten in the bath and opened the package when the phone rang. I put down the razor blade that was in my hand, and got out of the tub to find out who was calling. So here I am."

I spoke to April for fifteen minutes, and she decided that she would not harm herself – at least not before she saw me on Monday. As long as I cared enough to see her through her pain, she was willing to endure it a bit longer.

By the time I saw April on Monday, she was feeling a little bit better. Confronting death and choosing not to end it was a turning point for her. Ever so slowly, over the next two months, April's depression began to lift with the approaching spring. By the time she took her actuarial exams, she passed them. Against all odds, April pursued a very successful career, came to terms with her family, developed several close friends, and felt satisfied with her life. After two years, she stopped taking medication and stopped therapy.

Five years later, April called one day and asked if she could drop by my office for a consultation about some difficulties she was having with her boss at work. It took only fifteen minutes for us to work out how she could solve her dilemma with him. Afterward, we spent a few minutes discussing how her life had been during the prior five years. She had not had any recurrences of her depression, and was generally pleased with the way her life was turning out. Hers was truly a success story.

I was very pleased that I had ignored my better judgment and had taken April as a patient, despite my initial misgivings. From my experience with April I learned that categorizing people can be very helpful, but it can also make us lose sight of a person's uniqueness and strengths. I also considered, in a very sobering realization, that things could easily have turned out otherwise. Timing in life is everything, and sometimes, when we put off until later what we can do now, later is simply too late.

Judaism teaches us never to let opportunities to do positive things slip away. We have to grab those opportunities. Every day, we have chances to express our caring and empathy for others, but not necessarily in ways that make us comfortable. Every day, we can extend ourselves to be more than we are, and be truly Godly. If we keep our eyes, and our hearts open, we'll be aware of the opportunities that are sent our way that enable us to help others, and have the satisfaction of accomplishing more than we ever dreamed was possible.

On a Wing and a Prayer

Many years ago, Rabbi Dr. Ivan Lerner was the principal of a Jewish day school in California. Although the school followed the principles of observant Judaism, many of the students came from nonobservant homes. Their parents wanted them to attend the school primarily due to its academic excellence in secular studies. The administration and teachers hoped to show the students the beauty and importance of traditional Judaism. Needless to say, the gap between the students' and teachers' perspectives sometimes made it difficult to religiously inspire the students.

In August 1980, a vacancy for the position of second-grade teacher opened up. A number of applicants applied for the job, and one stood out from the rest. Connie Hodgson had been a teacher in the public school system of the District of Columbia and made an abrupt move to California. She was looking for work because her husband, an air force colonel, was transferred from Andrews Air Force Base in Washington to Edwards Air Force Base in the California desert. She loved teaching, and it was too late for her to get a teaching job in the public school system, so she thought she might be able to find work at a private school. She was hired to work at the Jewish day school and turned out to be a great teacher.

Tuning In

At the time, the United States was developing the shuttle space program, but the first shuttle had not yet been launched. Connie's husband John was in charge of its military components.

A few months into the school year, the school held a get-together for all of the teachers and their spouses. Connie's husband raced there from work, attired in his colonel's uniform bedecked with rows of decorations. Dr. Lerner, aware that he was being a bit brazen, approached Colonel Hodgson and requested, "Colonel, it would be so special if I could take our senior class to the air force base to see the shuttle."

The colonel replied, "You know, we are not set up to give tours to school kids. Only military brass and politicians are allowed out there. We can't really bring a school group to the base."

Undaunted, Dr. Lerner figured that if the colonel would only feel more connected to the school, he would change his mind. He scheduled two more teacher get-togethers. At the second one, the colonel approached him and offered, "I'll set up an opportunity for you to take the junior and senior classes to see the shuttle, but I want you to understand that this involves top-level security. The kids will all have to fill out background sheets and get security clearance."

Dr. Lerner joyfully replied, "That's fine. We'll do whatever you want."

When the children went home with their "security clearance" sheets a few weeks later, some of the parents panicked. They thought that the IRS or some similar government agency was investigating them! This was just a momentary problem, and they soon calmed down. Over the next days and weeks, a palpable excitement built among the students in the school. They felt special that they were going to do something that no one else was able to do. As the anticipated day drew near, the feeling of reverence built to a crescendo, akin to that of a peak religious experience.

The shuttle was assembled in a plant in Downey, California, a bit more than an hour's drive from the school. The students were required to be at school at 7:15 A.M. Even those students who usually

Everyone is a Messenger

came late to class were there early. It wasn't only the students who were caught up in the excitement about the shuttle. One of the Hebrew teachers had explained to Dr. Lerner numerous times why he needed to help chaperone the trip. Rabbi David was one of the senior boys' teachers, and Dr. Lerner agreed to let him accompany his class to see the shuttle.

In Southern California, getting students to wear normal clothing, such as pants and shirts, to school, is a struggle. Compliance with a school dress code which had even more rigorous requirements was a constant battle. Yet, the day of the class trip, the boys were formally dressed as if they were about to greet the Sabbath, and the girls were dressed as if they were ready for the High Holidays. The reverence that they had for the shuttle far surpassed the reverence they had for religion.

One of the school rules was that boys had to have their heads covered in school, and on all school trips, in compliance with Jewish custom. Soon after everyone was on the bus, Rabbi David tapped Dr. Lerner on the shoulder. "Look around the bus," he advised Dr. Lerner.

Dr. Lerner turned around and realized that only one of the boys was wearing a head covering. He felt very sad, got up, and told them, "C'mon, guys, you all know the school rules. Please put your *yarmulkes* (skullcaps) on. Don't be ashamed that you're Jewish."

The boys groaned, rolled their eyes to the ceiling, and grimaced. They reluctantly drew out their yarmulkes from where they had stuffed them in their pockets, and dropped them on their heads.

The bus continued on its way. A few minutes later, Dr. Lerner got another tap on his shoulder. Rabbi David sighed, "Look around again. The yarmulkes are gone."

This time Dr. Lerner got up and simply motioned to his head, in front of all of the students. The boys rolled their eyes, grimaced and groaned, and reluctantly slapped their yarmulkes on their heads again.

Tuning In

The third time that Rabbi David pointed out to Dr. Lerner that the yarmulkes were missing, Dr. Lerner replied, "You know, I feel really bad about this. But if these guys are so self-conscious and ashamed about being Jewish, I'm not going to make them neurotic right now. We've somehow failed to communicate to them why they should be proud of being Jews. I'm just not going to deal with it again right now."

Meanwhile, the bus pulled up outside the Rockwell plant, and the air police came to meet them. The police got on the bus, and checked that everyone had the one-day pass that they had been issued, as well as the other proper credentials.

The security guards wouldn't let the school bus enter the Rockwell plant. Everyone had to be transferred to an air force bus, with an air force police escort. All of this only continued to build reverence for the sight that the students were about to see. The air force bus then pulled up in front of the hangar, where an air force sergeant said, "I'd like all of you to exit the bus and stand along the yellow line outside. Someone will be here momentarily to meet you."

A military vehicle then pulled up, and a woman got out. She said, "Boys and girls, we don't do tours here. I don't know who you know, or how high up that person is, but you must have pulled some amazing strings. Since we don't do tours, one of our project engineers was willing to take the time to take you through our site. He will meet you inside that hangar there, where the shuttle is housed. Please go through that door and wait on the line inside that hangar. The engineer will come in to meet you from the other side."

As the group entered the hangar, their mouths were agape as they stared at the cavernous, aluminum structure with concrete floors. The acoustics were such that one could hear a pin drop. In the center stood the shuttle in all its glory, as wide as a 737, and immense in length. Lights were projected onto the tail of the shuttle, illuminating the American flag there. As the group stood in awe, gazing at this creation before its maiden voyage, a door across from the hangar opened. The dark figure of a person walking was discernible against the light.

Everyone is a Messenger

As he approached, it was evident that he had a beard. A moment later, they could see strings dangling out from his shirt. At that moment, Jerry Eisenman discerned who the person approaching them must be. He leaned over to Robby Roth and whispered, "How did they let a rabbi in here?!"

Robby Roth, a very bright boy, suggested, "Maybe he's a chaplain."

As the man got closer, his ritual fringes seemed to grow larger and larger until he stood in front of the group. Instead of being a chaplain or rabbi, the tag on his clothing proclaimed, "Dr. Sheldon Levi, Project Director, Inertial Guidance Systems, NASA Space Shuttle."

At that moment, Dr. Lerner's heart was beating with joy, and he exclaimed to himself, "Thank you, God. This is the best!"

Simultaneously, every boy was facing Sheldon Levi, trying to figure out how to surreptitiously retrieve his yarmulke, have it migrate up the back of his shirt, and place it on his head. Within seconds, every boy proudly sported his yarmulke.

Dr. Levi then addressed the group. "You know, boys, we were very busy here today. When I heard that a yeshiva (Jewish religious school) was coming, I had to make time in my schedule to show you around."

Dr. Levi then led the group inside the shuttle, and explained its various components. As military brass walked through the hangar, they all greeted him, "Hello, Shelly." It was obvious to the students that he was a very important person.

As the group stood in the cockpit of the shuttle, Jerry Eisenman was still in shock at seeing an unabashed, obviously observant Jew, working in such an elite position. He tentatively posed a question to Dr. Levi, "Are there…a lot of people like…you, who work here?"

Dr. Levi looked at him, and without hesitating replied, "Son, this place is full of astrophysicists."

Jerry tried again. "No…I didn't mean that. I meant…"

Dr. Levi understood quickly, smiled, and came to his aid. "You mean – *frum* (Orthodox Jewish)?"

Tuning In

With that, Dr. Levi put his arm around Jerry and confided, "If it wouldn't be for us frummies (Orthodox Jews), they couldn't make this thing fly."

At that point, Dr. Levi added, "We normally daven mincha (say the afternoon prayer service) in hangar 31. Seeing as how all of you are in the shuttle hangar today, I decided that we'll all *daven mincha* here today instead."

At that moment, as if on cue, an air force sergeant walked in, his arms laden with Jewish prayer books. The school group prayed the afternoon service with Dr. Sheldon Levi and with his colleagues who were working on the Enterprise under the starboard wing of the shuttle that day. (The Enterprise is now on display at the Aeronautics and Space Museum in Washington, D. C.)

Suffice it to say, the day turned out to be a great success on many counts, not the least of which was to show the students that they could be proud of being Jewish.

Brother, Can You Spare A...Friend?

By most people's standards, Robbie Hochberg lived a very privileged life. He had grown up in a wealthy city in Florida, full of private golf courses and swim clubs. His father was a doctor and his mother was a housewife, who spent much of her time taking care of Robbie and his younger brother when they were very young. When they started school full-time, she spent hours every week talking to her friends, shopping, and going out to restaurants.

Robbie's parents divorced when he was eight. Robbie lived with his mother, and his father continued to see or speak to Robbie every week. For many years, Robbie loved going to his friends' homes after school and on weekends. These houses were incredibly lavish, and were filled with the latest toys, electronics and gadgets. One family even had a full library, where removing a certain book from the bookshelf resulted in the room opening up into a casino! A father of another friend was a car dealer and drove a new car every month. About six teenagers in each of his high school classes had had cosmetic surgery, as had the majority of his friends' parents. Even his mother had subjected herself to the artistic knife.

As Robbie grew older, he began to tire of his friends' latest technological toys, and was repulsed by the fathers who got divorced and remarried beautiful young women. These trophy women were often not much older than his friends.

Tuning In

Having opulent homes, expensive toys, and beautiful women were the benchmarks of success in his neighborhood, despite the fact that most of the children ended up with divorced parents, or with parents who had – at best – tenuous relationships with their children.

It was expected that every one of Robbie's friends would get a car for his sixteenth birthday, the main point of which was to allow the teen to drive to high school and impress everyone with his expensive acquisitions. A father's worth was assessed by his job, his income, the kind of home he had, the model car he drove, and the country club to which he belonged. His sons were judged by the kind of cars they drove and how gorgeous their girlfriends were. Despite finding this crass materialism somewhat abhorrent, Robbie had no other model to which to aspire and he bought into it lock, stock, and barrel.

Robbie's Jewish identity was every bit as superficial as the rest of his identity. In his community, Judaism was purely cultural, and Jews tried to have the best that liberal Western society had to offer. Those boys who had bar mitzvah ceremonies marking their attainment of Jewish adulthood were relieved not to have to attend synagogue ever again. Needless to say, Robbie wanted no part of this form of Judaism.

He went away to college where he became a serious party animal. He exclusively dated Gentile women because the culturally Jewish women he knew from his background were not his type. They were far too materialistic and wanted to marry in order to climb the next rung on the social ladder. It was not long before he met Christie, a stunning young woman who grew up with no religious background, who had been raised in a Christian family. The two of them became seriously involved with one another over the next two years. Part of their enjoyment of each other was sharing heavy drinking every Friday night, and taking Ecstasy and other recreational drugs on a regular basis with their friends. Toward the end of his junior year in college, Robbie decided that he was in love with Christie and he planned to propose to her.

Around that time, his father called and asked Robbie if he was planning to come home for the annual Passover *seder* (a special festival meal that recounts the Jews' ancient history and celebrates their exodus from Egypt).

"No," Robbie replied.

"Why not?" his father inquired, a bit stunned.

"Because I have sat through enough of those ridiculous seders for two lifetimes. There's nothing sacred about the kind of seders we have. All we do is try to hurry up as much as possible so that we can get to the meal." Robbie had recognized during his childhood that this kind of behavior was the antithesis of sanctity.

His father continued, "What do you think that Passover is about?"

Robbie responded, "It's about getting out of Egypt."

His father persisted, "How is that relevant to your life?"

Robbie replied, without too much conviction, "I guess that if it weren't for Passover, we'd still be in Egypt."

His father continued, "What if I told you that Passover is not only about physical enslavement? It's about anything that enslaves us physically, morally, emotionally…For example, nicotine, or caffeine, or judging others, or self-doubt, are all forms of enslavement."

Robbie was astounded. "Wow! Where did you hear that?"

"Would you believe that this is how Orthodox Jews view Passover?"

Robbie replied, "No."

His father retorted, "Well, they do. I've been learning with an Orthodox rabbi and this is how he explained Passover to me…. Now do you want to come join me for the seder?"

Robbie demurred. "No, thanks, I'd rather go to Cancun with Christie."

A few days later, Robbie received a parcel in the mail from his father. It was *The Complete Idiot's Guide to Understanding Judaism*. He read it and was impressed by the personal growth that the holidays represented, as well as by the deeper meanings of life that were reflected by the rituals that he had formerly thought were arcane and irrelevant. Nonetheless, Robbie continued living exactly as he had before, although a seed had been planted in his mind that maybe there was more to Judaism than he had previously assumed.

Tuning In

Robbie graduated college and got a high-pressured sales job that had the potential to reap lucrative commissions. Meanwhile, Christie got a job in another city where she had a chance to make her fortune. Money triumphed over the relationship and they agreed to see other people.

Robbie got into his next relationship. This time he had an intense relationship with a Catholic woman.

One day, a friend called and asked him to donate blood for someone in the Jewish community. Robbie was among thousands of Jews who showed up. Robbie had been working out in the gym, as he had for the prior ten years, in the hope that he could sculpt his body into Adonis-like perfection. He joined the long line of blood donors. He stood wearing his tank top and shorts and read a novel. The young man in front of him was roughly Robbie's age and wore a skullcap. Sammy turned around and introduced himself. Robbie felt repulsed. He did not want to engage in conversation with Sammy because he assumed that this Orthodox Jew would be an idiot.

Sammy, however, was not easily dissuaded, and it was soon apparent that Sammy and Robbie had much in common. It turned out that they both had grown up in the same city and were from assimilated Jewish backgrounds. Unlike Robbie, however, Sammy had become observant a few years earlier, when he was in his twenties. In the course of their conversation, Sammy informed Robbie about the local synagogue and invited him for a Sabbath meal.

Robbie had never heard about Sabbath meals and immediately declined the invitation.

Robbie made the "mistake" of giving Sammy his telephone number. Sammy, for his part, pursued Robbie with a phone call every week to wish him a good Sabbath and invited him for a meal. Eventually, Robbie made a point to see if Sammy's number showed up on his caller ID when the phone rang. If it did, Robbie refused to pick up the phone.

In time, Robbie met an older man who observed, "You know something, you seem like the kind of person who would enjoy the

Everyone is a Messenger

beginner's service at the local Orthodox synagogue. It's called Beth Israel." Robbie recognized the name of the synagogue as the same one that Sammy had been recommending for months. Robbie called Sammy back a few days later and went to his first Sabbath meal.

At the meal, Robbie began grilling a rabbi there about all kinds of theological matters that had bothered him. The rabbi replied, after hearing one of the questions, "You know, that's a great question. You should go to a yeshiva."

Robbie inquired, "What's a yeshiva?"

The rabbi explained that a yeshiva is a school where Jewish men study Judaism. Although Robbie wasn't inclined to investigate a yeshiva, he proceeded to attend the synagogue intermittently on the Sabbath over the next six years on his way to the park to meet friends. Robbie was impressed by the lack of focus on materialism, their emphasis on raising children and living in emotionally healthy families, and their dedication to building a quality life. Still, Robbie did nothing to change his own life to make it more like theirs.

One night, Robbie got caught in a massive traffic jam. He picked up *The Complete Idiot's Guide to Understanding Judaism* as he sat waiting – the same book that his father had sent him years earlier that had sat unnoticed in Robbie's car all that time. The book spontaneously opened to the section on giving charity, and Robbie read about the different ways of giving. The book said that Judaism believes that there are various levels of giving charity. The least preferred ways are to give to someone in need in a way that both the giver and the receiver see each other. It is better to give charity in a way that preserves people's anonymity. The highest level, though, is to offer someone the opportunity to earn his own living, and thereby retain his dignity. The book commented that there is even a higher level of charity than this, and that is to befriend someone in need. As soon as Robbie finished reading that paragraph, the traffic jam eased, and he put the book down. As he continued to drive, he processed what he had read.

He soon noticed that he needed gas, and stopped at a gas station in a crime-ridden section of town. He went inside the station to pay for the gas, and when he returned to his car, he noticed a quite disheveled, homeless black man wearing camouflage fatigues standing next to his car. Robbie noted that it was dark and cold outside, and he felt frightened standing in such a dangerous place. He approached the man with the sole plan he knew of how to confront the situation.

"Sorry, man," Robbie apologized, "I don't have any money."

The vagrant, who had previously seemed off-balance and intoxicated, suddenly straightened. He looked Robbie in the eye, and perfectly articulated, "Look at the assumption you just made about me. You presumed that because I'm a black man that I'm asking you for money."

Robbie was shocked, but didn't know how to respond. He was quaking inside with fear. "What do you want?" he asked the man.

The man continued, "It's not what I want, it's what you need."

"Hunh?" Robbie mustered.

The vagrant persisted, "What are you doing here?"

Robbie responded easily, "It's a gas station. I'm getting gas."

The vagrant didn't accept the answer. He stared Robbie straight in the eye. "No, man, I don't mean, what are you doing here," and he pointed to the ground. He spread his arms wide and threw his head back, looking up at the universe. "I mean here. What are you doing here?"

Robbie was stunned. He managed another, "Hunh?"

For a few moments, Robbie stood petrified of this strange man in camouflage. He hoped the man would just leave him alone. Finally, Robbie said meekly, "I don't know what I'm doing here."

The homeless man retorted, "That's your biggest problem. If you don't know what you're doing down here, that's your biggest danger."

Robbie, still misunderstanding the man's intentions, stepped back and said, "I know how to take care of myself." He prepared to fight or to defend himself.

The man calmly said, "Look at the assumption you just made about me. I pose no threat to you." The stranger shuffled his feet, moved back to a shaky pose, and his eyes glazed over. In a softer voice he revealed, "Unfortunately, your first assessment of me was right. I'm a crack addict and I was looking for money to buy my next hit." He proceeded to recount to Robbie how he was the only one of his peers to graduate high school because he wanted to make something of himself. After high school, he enlisted in the army. When he left the army after a few years, he returned to see his family and old friends. He soon was partying regularly and was addicted to crack.

The man's menacing expression had softened, and he appeared more and more despondent as he told Robbie his tale of woe. Soon, the man stopped talking and averted his eyes from Robbie's. As he hung his head in shame, his eyes misted over, and before Robbie could process what was happening, the man began to sob.

"You were right. I was looking for money. But what I need more than money or my next hit of crack," he said, picking up his head and again looking Robbie in the eye, "is a friend."

Robbie wasn't prepared to become this man's friend. He was so unsettled by this stranger's baring his soul full of pain that Robbie took a bill from his wallet and pressed it into the man's hand. The man clasped the crumpled note. Burdened by the confrontation with his ruined life, the man shuffled away from the car.

Robbie heaved a sigh of relief, hastily climbed into his car, and sped away. At the next traffic light, he opened the book that he had been reading, and reread the last words that he had read moments before, "The highest form of charity is to be a friend to someone in need."

Robbie's mind replayed with total clarity, like a flashback in a movie, the scene that had just transpired. He felt emotionally overwhelmed and wracked with anxiety. What did it say about him that he was unwilling to offer his friendship to a man who was down and out? What kind of person was he, that he was only willing to offer money (and a trifling amount, at that) instead of anything of himself to someone in need? He looked back at the gas station to see if he could make it up to the man. The man was nowhere to be seen. He had simply vanished into the frigid, dark night. Robbie was unable to deal with the meaning that he attributed to his actions during the bizarre encounter. Could

Tuning In

he truly be as crass and self-centered as the people whom he despised from his childhood? He quickly drove away.

Robbie never again picked up the book on Judaism, as it challenged his entire worldview. It was simply too threatening for Robbie to delve into questions of who he had become, and whether he needed to change himself in order to be a better person.

A few months later, Robbie was about to land a very lucrative contract with a client when he had an intense moment of clarity about himself and his life. He walked calmly into his boss' office.

"I'm quitting my job," Robbie informed his boss.

The boss asked, "What happened with that great account you were about to land?"

Robbie replied, "It went perfectly. I got the account. I'm going to give it to Jim."

The boss refused his resignation, and wanted to investigate if Robbie was taking mind-altering drugs. "Why in the world do you want to quit?" his boss prodded.

Robbie had a flashback of growing up in a ridiculously materialistic community. Board meetings were more important to most of the fathers than birthday parties were. Families had crumbled around him as fathers were invested more in their wallets than in their wives and children. Robbie had no respect for his boss who regularly worked thirteen- and fourteen-hour days while he raked in half-a-million dollars a year. How did it feel to be his three young children who were growing up without having a relationship with their father? What kind of man had his boss become, that he wasn't pained by the lack of a relationship with his wife and children?

Robbie felt sad for himself, and for all of them. He thought about what most of the people he had known were really chasing. It was Hollywood, movie stars, fame, fortune, and all of the illusions of comfort, success, love and security that they symbolized. Everyone wanted to be like these people, yet the truly rich and famous, the movie stars, the glamour queens, and others who had achieved the American definitions of "success" were generally miserable in their real lives. They weren't fulfilled and happy. To the contrary, it was depressing striving for their goals, only to discover during a mid-life or end-life crisis that they really didn't deliver.

Robbie decided to quit not only his job, but also the society that he had known for so many years. He quoted Lily Tomlin, the comedienne, to his boss, "The problem with the rat race is that even if you win, you're still a rat."

His boss reiterated his refusal to accept Robbie's resignation and urged him not to make any rash decisions.

Robbie went back to his office and decided to move forward with his convictions. As soon as he could get his affairs in order, he would move to Colorado and work on the ski slopes during the winters. He would camp out and hike in the parks and forests during the summers. He would eke out a living there in a way that he would be happy.

Elated with his decision, he called his girlfriend and best friend and gushed about his plans. They both asked, "When do we leave?" Robbie figured that it would take a month or two to put his affairs in order, and then they would all be free to live out their dream.

As Robbie liquidated his assets, his father called, hoping to dissuade him from his seemingly impulsive decision. "Son, I understand why you are doing what you are doing. But instead of trying to run away from a misguided world, why don't you try to change it?"

Robbie appreciated his father's wisdom and advice, but didn't see how it applied to him at that moment. "I'm just one man," he told his father.

His father was not deterred. "Well, I know a group of people with the same moral convictions that you are espousing who are trying to change the world."

"Who are they?" Robbie inquired.

"They are a bunch of Orthodox Jews who live in Jerusalem, led by a rabbi who wants to make the world a more meaningful and moral place. They want a world where a man's value is not determined by decimal points but by his contributions to society."

Tuning In

It was not long before Robbie discovered that there was a one-month program in Jerusalem at a yeshiva dedicated to these goals. He decided to postpone his move to Colorado by a month while he checked things out halfway across the world.

That was more than two years ago. Robbie is still in Jerusalem, doing his part to make the world a better place.

Part III:
Having Children

The Right Place at the Right Time

I was reaching the end of a long speaking tour on the West Coast of the United States, and a rabbi asked if I would be willing to add a few cities to my itinerary. He told me about a small Jewish community that was off the beaten path that would love if I could come and address them. I was traveling with my family and we agreed to make a detour to the picturesque town overlooking the Pacific Ocean.

The organizers of the event, Stanley and his wife Marcie, offered us hospitality in their Victorian house, where they made us feel very much at home. Both were energetic, in their early thirties, and eager to learn as much as they could about traditional Judaism. Neither had grown up in Jewishly enriched homes, and they were making up for lost time.

As a thank-you for hosting us, I wanted to give them some Judaica books that I had recently written. Fortunately for me, my tour had been so successful that none of them remained. The only books that I had left were those they already owned, plus a secular book on pregnancy that I had co-authored (*What Your Unborn Baby Wants You to Know*). I was reluctant to offer it to Marcie, as it seemed a bit presumptuous and intrusive to give a book on pregnancy to a woman whom I barely knew. I decided to simply show Marcie the titles that I had left and asked her to pick any that were of interest to her. She told me that she had the

Tuning In

others, and would like the book on pregnancy. I felt bad that she was taking that book because I had nothing else to give her.

A few minutes later, our family was on the way to the airport. I kissed Marcie goodbye and wished her and Stanley well.

A year and a half later, I was preparing to give a talk at a women's seminary in Jerusalem, when a familiar face appeared before me. Her face was aglow, framed by a stylish hat, and her bright eyes shone in my direction.

"You probably don't remember me, but my husband and I hosted you at our home," she reminded me. "My name is Marcie Haber, and my husband is Stanley." In a split second, I had made the connection.

"What are you doing here?" I exclaimed.

Marcie smiled. "Stanley and I decided that we wanted to visit Israel, partly to study Judaism, partly to see the country. This is our first trip here. I'm studying at this seminary, and he's studying in a men's yeshiva."

Since I was about to start my talk, I didn't have much time to catch up with Marcie. "I'd love to have the two of you come to my home for Friday night dinner next week. Would that be possible?"

Marcie beamed and nodded.

"Great," I replied, "here's my address and phone number. We look forward to seeing you and Stanley."

The following week, Marcie and Stanley arrived with their one-year-old baby just in time to light the Sabbath candles. As the sun began its descent, and the Sabbath slowly made its appearance, my family escorted them on their first trip to the holiest site for Jews today. Thousands of Jews poured into the Old City as we made our way down countless stairs to the Western Wall. Before we approached the Wall, we stood above and overlooked the Temple Mount, where the two Jewish Temples once stood. We watched the crowd of thousands of Jews singing and swaying as they ushered in the Sabbath. It took our breath away. The men then went to the men's side to pray and Marcie, her baby Rena, and I went to the ladies' side.

Having Children

Praying next to Marcie was very distracting. Not a minute went by that some young lady, seasoned mother, or grandmother didn't come over and play with Rena! They cooed at her, commented about how beautiful she was, played peek-a-boo with her, and held her while Marcie tried to concentrate on the prayers.

Rena was indeed a beautiful baby, with brilliant blue eyes, full, apple-red cheeks, a winning smile, and an engaging expression. She was delighted by all of the attention she received, and the ladies around her were only too happy to lavish more on her.

An hour later, the beautiful singing of the Sabbath prayers was over, and we made our way back home. As we waited for the rest of our guests to arrive, Marcie unbundled Rena, and told me nonchalantly that she wanted to thank me for the role I played in Rena's health.

I was setting out napkins at the time and thought that I had misunderstood what Marcie had said. I stopped what I was doing, turned to face her, and asked, "What did I have to do with Rena?"

By now, Rena was happily cruising next to my coffee table, tasting every second or third object that she found.

Marcie looked me in the eyes and smiled. "Do you remember when you came to my house; you gave me a book that you wrote on pregnancy?"

Of course I remembered. I still felt apologetic about it.

Marcie continued, "You didn't know it, but the day that you came, I had just gone to my doctor and found out that I was pregnant with Rena. When I got your book, I opened it to the chapter on birth defects. One of the first things that I read was that Retin-A, something that I had been using on my face, causes birth defects when pregnant women use it. My doctor hadn't told me that. I stopped using it immediately. So, I thank you for your part in helping me have a healthy baby."

In retrospect, what I thought was an unfortunate lack of suitable Judaica books turned out to be the greatest gift of all, arranged by a Giver Who knew exactly what Marcie, and Rena, needed to receive.

Nothing is Inconceivable for God

Julio and Sarah were in their mid-twenties when they got married. They lived in Buenos Aires, where they ran a clothing store together. Three years later, they decided that it was time to start a family. A year later, Sarah still had not conceived, so they went to a doctor for a fertility evaluation. Much to their shock, Julio was diagnosed as being severely infertile. At the time, no medical interventions were available that could assist them in their quest to have a child. Nevertheless, Julio never gave up hope. Over the next two years, he tried to obtain a more promising diagnosis as new infertility interventions became available. In all, Julio consulted seven more specialists. They all viewed his situation as hopeless and recommended adopting if the couple wanted children.

At the time, few infertility resources were available in Argentina. A friend advised them to consult a rabbi who was well-known for helping infertile Jewish couples. Julio and Sarah considered themselves modern people, and thought it was a bit strange in the twentieth century to be consulting a spiritual guide for help with medical problems. Yet, they deeply wanted to have a baby and didn't think it could hurt to try this route.

First, the rabbi checked the *mezuzot* from their house. The Bible commands Jews to affix small parchments, on which are written biblical verses in Hebrew, on the entrances and doorways of their

Tuning In

homes. These parchments are known as mezuzot. When mezuzot are not written properly, one does not fulfill the commandment to affix mezuzot, and the members of the family may encounter difficulties in their lives. The rabbi checked the mezuzot and discovered that every letter *bayt* (analogous to the letter B from the English alphabet) was written improperly. Unlike in the English alphabet, Hebrew letters also have mystical meanings. The letter bayt is shaped like, and also symbolizes, a home. Bayt, similar to the Hebrew word *bayit*, means "home." The rabbi corrected the mistakes and gave them the mezuzot to put back on the doorposts of their home.

The rabbi also checked Julio's *tefillin*. Tefillin are small leather boxes that contain biblical verses written on parchment. The Bible commands men to place them around the head and on the arm using attached leather straps. Men do this customarily when they say the morning prayers. If the verses are not written properly, tefillin, like mezuzot, are invalid. Julio's tefillin were problematic and could not be repaired. He purchased a new pair.

Initially, Julio and Sarah were hopeful that this would mystically remedy their infertility problem. Unfortunately, Sarah still did not conceive. The following year, a kabbalistic rabbi came to their town and the couple went to see him. The rabbi asked Julio to tell him their Hebrew names. The rabbi looked perplexed, then asked, "Who are David, Bella and Rivka?"

Julio replied, "They are my grandfather and my wife's two grandmothers." Grandma Rivka was still alive and in her eighties at the time. Grandpa David and Grandma Bella had been deceased for many years.

The Rabbi nodded, then proceeded to tell the couple all sorts of things about themselves. When he finished, he asked, "Do you have any questions?"

Sarah asked, with some trepidation in her voice, "Will Julio and I ever have children?"

The rabbi responded, "Yes, you will."

Next she asked, "Should we adopt?"

Having Children

The rabbi replied, "If you'd like to, you can, but you will have your own children in the merit of Julio's grandfather and your grandmothers."

For the next two years, Julio and Sarah started each monthly cycle hoping that she would conceive, then had their hopes dashed two weeks later when they realized that she still was not pregnant. Finally, they consulted a doctor who informed them that a new fertility technique (ICSI) was available. It afforded men who had previously been considered irremediably infertile the possibility of fathering children.

Meanwhile, the couple contacted a very old, very wise rabbi in Jerusalem and asked him their $64,000 question.

"Don't worry, don't worry," the rabbi assured them, "you will have your own children."

Despite his assurances, Julio and Sarah were already married for seven years and she had still never conceived. It was hard not to worry.

After the rabbi's pronouncement, Sarah looked into Julio's warm, dark eyes. Her own eyes, with a sadness behind them that never seemed to go away, silently asked him, "Do you think it's really possible?"

Julio gazed at her, "I hope so," he said, wanting to reassure her, wanting to reassure himself.

Julio's urologist then recommended that he see a male-infertility specialist in New York. Julio made the expensive and lengthy trip only to be told that the doctors could not help him. Instead, they referred Julio to an infertility clinic in Los Angeles where ICSI was routinely performed. After making the trip there, the specialist told Julio that he and his wife could avail themselves of the ICSI procedure when they were ready.

A few months later, Julio lost his job due to a recession. Instead of viewing it as a catastrophe, he and Sarah collected their life savings of $20,000 that they had amassed from investing in the stock market. They decided to reinvest it in two airline tickets to the United States and fees for infertility treatment.

Tuning In

During this time, Julio and Sarah decided to have their Jewish marriage document, known as a ketubah, checked for mistakes. It turned out that when Julio had given the document to Sarah during their wedding ceremony, her uncle had witnessed it. Jewish law prohibits relatives from being legal witnesses to an event. Thus, Julio had to give a new ketubah to his wife in the presence of two valid witnesses.

Then came the next spiritual prescription. Sarah started going to the Jewish ritual bath, known as a mikvah, every month. The Bible commands Jewish couples not to have sexual relations from the time the woman gets her period every month until after the bleeding ceases and she subsequently immerses herself in a mikvah. Just prior to immersing, the woman must make sure that she is scrupulously clean so that nothing will intervene between her body and the water that will spiritually elevate her. After immersing, the woman and her husband may resume having physical relations until the next time that she gets her period. Sarah had heard that other women in her family had performed this ancient ritual, and figured she had nothing to lose by trying it, too.

Finally, Julio went to see a rabbi from Paris who came to town. Before telling the rabbi why he came to see him, Julio wrote his and his wife's Hebrew names on a piece of paper for the rabbi to see, since some rabbis can glean valuable, hidden information about people by studying their Hebrew names. The rabbi read the names and said, "You don't have children and you also don't have a job. May the Almighty bless you with both." The rabbi indicated that it was time for the next person to enter the room.

Julio felt frustrated and angry. Here he had expected to find an empathic ear, a person to whom he could pour out all his pain, after seven years of this nightmare. Instead, all he got was a quick brush off, and he was hurried out of room with a patronizing response the rabbi could have told anybody. How could this rabbi know what he needed without speaking to him at length? He felt like a fool for even coming and wasting his time once again. He was given a quick blessing and had

Having Children

no reason to believe that it would invoke Divine assistance. Julio left without telling anyone about his encounter with this rabbi.

It took Julio and Sarah eight months from the time he lost his job to make the trip to Los Angeles. Shortly before they left, Sarah immersed in the mikveh just after a pregnant woman had done so. That was considered to be a good omen for pregnancy.

Every Sabbath, Jews around the world read a designated portion of the Bible in the synagogue. The Torah portion that was read the week that Julio and Sarah traveled to the United States was one that discusses the blessings that the Jewish people will receive if they keep the commandments of the Bible. It says that they will be blessed among all of the nations of the world and that there will be no barren men, women or animals among them.

When Julio and Sarah started treatment, they realized that what the Almighty denied him He gave her in abundance! Sarah produced nineteen eggs (a woman usually produces only one each month), of which ten fertilized.

A few days later, the doctor implanted four embryos in Sarah. A week later, the couple returned to Buenos Aires full of hope. Two weeks went by, and then Sarah started bleeding. They were very worried and called her doctor who told her to stay in bed. When the profuse bleeding persisted, they went to the doctor on Rosh Ha'Shana, the Jewish New Year.

Sarah's heart sank. She had hoped upon hope this new year would be a new start for them – the beginning of their family. Instead, the familiar bleeding that signaled the death of potential life, consumed her. Would there ever be an end to this suffering? *This kind of emotional pain is more than I can possibly bear,* she thought to herself. *How many times can our hearts be broken? How much longer can we have the strength to wake up and go through the day, without having a new, precious life to give to?*

After they arrived at the doctor's office, he performed an ultrasound and, lo and behold, showed the couple a tiny embryo on the monitor! They were ecstatic, but now they were riding an emotional roller

Tuning In

coaster. First they had been worried that Sarah might bleed to death – now they discovered that she was creating a new life!

After Rosh Ha'Shana ended, they called Grandma Rivka to share the wonderful news with her. She was thrilled, but not entirely surprised. She had been praying every night for a long time that Julio and Sarah should have a child. Could her prayers have been the merit that the rabbi had predicted would help them have a baby?

As thrilled as they were to finally be pregnant, everything was not rosy. Grandma Rivka's health started declining as Sarah's pregnancy advanced. A month before the baby was born, Grandma Rivka passed away. It seemed as if once the new baby was nearly born, Grandma Rivka had finished her final task here and could go to her eternal reward.

Julio and Sarah were emotionally and physically spent by the time their baby daughter was delivered by Cesarean section. It all happened so fast, that Julio couldn't believe his eyes. This baby that they had gone to the ends of the earth, and beyond, physically and spiritually, to bring into this world was finally here. Julio watched as the doctors removed this tiny creature from his wife's womb and proceeded to bring her to life. Moments later, the nurse put the swaddled baby into Julio's strong, but quavering, arms. All he saw was a shock of dark hair, and a beatific face, with eyes that were squinting to take in this new amazing world where she had suddenly found herself. Julio's eyes filled with tears of joy so quickly, that is all he saw of his newborn daughter, as he hugged her to his chest and welcomed her into his life. As his wife awoke from her anesthesia, he had no words to tell her of the miracle that had arrived. He placed the tiny new life on his wife's chest, as she wept.

Julio went home from the hospital, put on his tefillin as he did every weekday, and prayed. When he reached the prayers that describe how the Jewish people crossed the Reed Sea after their exodus from Egypt, he recited the words, "The Lord is above all praises, He makes miracles," and then broke down and sobbed. He recognized that the Almighty had made a miracle for him just as He had done

Having Children

for the newborn Jewish nation thousands of years earlier when they were pursued by their Egyptian captors. Just like the Israelites who perceived the Divine Presence at the Reed Sea, Julio saw the Hand of God when his daughter was born.

On the first Sabbath after the baby was born, Julio was called to the Torah (Bible) reading in the synagogue. He named his new baby Rivka after her maternal grandmother, who had recently passed away. She was given her second name, Bella, after her paternal grandmother. In Hebrew, every letter has a numerical value, such that alef equals one, bayt equals two, and so on. This Hebrew numerology is known as gemmatria. Adding the numerical values of the letters in words can reveal deep mystical insights. The numerical value of the Hebrew letters that spell the name Bella is thirty-seven. The baby was born thirty-seven years after her paternal grandmother passed away.

The seven weeks between the holiday of Passover and Shavuot (also known as the Feast of Weeks) is a special time for Jews. During this period some nineteen-hundred years ago, twenty-four-thousand pairs of disciples of one of the greatest Torah scholars, Rabbi Akiva, perished in a plague. This left the Jewish people almost bereft of Torah scholars. On the thirty-third day of this period, known as *Lag B'Omer*, the lethal plague stopped. A very great sage, Rabbi Shimon Bar Yochai, died that same day (although not that year). He declared Lag B'Omer a day of tremendous joy and good tidings for the Jewish people. He promised Jews who celebrated the anniversary of his death that he would intercede on their behalf with the One Above to help actualize their wishes.

Rivka Bella was born on Lag B'Omer. It was now nine years after the couple had married. Rivka Bella was born on a Tuesday, a day that is considered to be the most blessed of the weekdays. When the book of Genesis describes how the Creator brought the world into being, it says that He surveyed His creations each day. On the third day, He saw His creation and twice proclaimed that it was good. What an auspicious time for this beautiful little girl to come into the world!

Tuning In

Ten months later, Julio and Sarah took Rivka to the rabbi who was visiting from Paris. The rabbi asked the Almighty to bless the little girl and was very happy to see her miraculous appearance in the world. He also believed that God's miraculous actions in her conception were brought about, in part, by the merit of his very pious grandfather.

The rabbi asked, "How long are you married, and how old is your baby?"

The couple told him, "We are married ten years, and our baby is now ten-months old."

The rabbi summoned a man who was outside the room. The rabbi told the man in Hebrew, "Here is a couple that has been married for ten years and they now have a ten-month-old baby. What greater proof do you need of God's existence?" (In other words, what else besides a God who rules nature could overcome the circumstances that wouldn't let them have a child all those years?)

When the stranger exited, the rabbi informed Julio and Sarah, "Now it's time for a baby boy."

Julio was thunderstruck. In a flash, he thought about his encounters with rabbis who, years before, had assured him that he would have children. His good fortune in having his daughter was something he almost dared never hope for again. Being told that he would have a second child made him feel humbled by the abundant, undeserved goodness that he hoped to receive.

The couple soon returned to Los Angeles where the doctors had frozen their embryos. The doctor thawed four of the remaining six. Miraculously, they all thawed in good condition. (Frozen embryos often don't survive when they are brought back to normal temperature.) The doctor implanted all four into Sarah's womb, and the couple left the next day for Buenos Aires. Again, the interminable wait began.

Fourteen very long days later, they got back the lab results. Sarah was not pregnant – she was very pregnant. A month later, they learned that they were expecting twins.

Having Children

The rabbi came from France and saw Julio in the synagogue a week before their scheduled appointment. Before Julio had a chance to share the good news, the rabbi greeted him gleefully.

"Congratulations, your wife is pregnant." He then gave Sarah a blessing for an easy birth. Sarah had a healthy, uneventful second pregnancy and the couple looked forward to the arrival of the new lives growing in Sarah's womb.

On the eve of the Sabbath, Sarah's water broke suddenly and she went into labor. Julio had to rush her to the hospital, where a healthy baby boy and girl were soon delivered by Cesarean section. That Sabbath the Torah portion that was read contained the Ten Commandments and the *Shema* prayer. The Shema prayer proclaims that God is the only force that exists in the world.

The following Sabbath was a momentous one for Julio and Sarah. Since the twins were born on the Sabbath, their son's *brit milah*, circumcision on the eighth day of life, would also take place on this holiest of days, along with the naming ceremony for their baby daughter. Julio was called to the Torah and named his daughter Muriel (the light of God). And, in gratitude for Julio's grandfather's merits, which seemed to play a significant role in their son's birth, Julio and Sarah named their baby boy David.

That Sabbath's Torah portion promised the Jewish people that there would be no barren men, women or children among them if they collectively observed the Torah. In the normally noisy synagogue one could hear a pin drop when the rabbi announced that the congregants were witnessing the fulfillment of a Torah prophecy that they read that morning.

At that point, only two of Sarah and Julio's frozen embryos remained. Unlike the other embryos, these only had two cells, and were not likely to produce another pregnancy. Also, the doctor had strongly advised the couple against trying to have another baby. Their three children had been delivered by Cesarean section, and the doctor considered it risky for Sarah to have another pregnancy. He believed that, given the fact that Sarah's abdomen and uterus had been cut twice

Tuning In

already, her muscles were too weak to withstand another pregnancy and would likely be stretched beyond their limit, preventing her from carrying a baby to term.

The rabbi came from France when the twins were two-months old. Their first trip out of the house was to see him and get his blessing. Needless to say, the rabbi was very pleased to see the couple literally loaded with three very young children.

He returned again some months later and mentioned to Julio and Sarah, "There is hope that you will have another baby boy." Several doctors had already told them that they had no chance of conceiving without ICSI, and the couple was not interested in going for more fertility treatments. Julio and Sarah were also quite happy and busy with the three children they had. The doctor's warning about the risks involved in another pregnancy still lingered in their minds.

Before Sarah and Julio realized it, the twins turned a year old. Soon after the Jewish High Holidays, Sarah broke the news that she was pregnant again. Julio's first reaction was to dismiss her and say that the pregnancy test that she had bought at the drug store must have given a false positive result. Julio was convinced that there was no way that eight fine doctors could be wrong about the fact that she would never get pregnant without intervention.

Two days later, Sarah called from the doctor's office to tell Julio that not only was she pregnant, the pregnancy was already two months along!

"So much for doctors," Julio thought. Here they had spent their life savings and more years than they cared to think about seeking the best medical care in the world, and hanging on doctor's opinions as if they were gospel truth. Now they were finding out, through their firsthand experience, that the Creator of science and medicine was ruling their lives.

The rabbi flew in from France a few months later. He sat behind a desk while Julio went to meet him with his two daughters, while Sarah was in another room chasing their little boy. Before Julio had a chance to open his mouth, the rabbi turned to Julio and said, "Your wife is

Having Children

pregnant! The baby will be a boy and he will be born close to Passover. May Sarah have an easy birth."

The day before Passover, Sarah went into labor and gave birth to a baby boy.

Julio asked himself why, after so many years of infertility, God blessed him and Sarah with children. He came to the conclusion, which has been reached by others in similar predicaments, that perhaps it could be to show that God hears the prayers of even simple people, not just the most pious and righteous individuals. While it doesn't hurt to be such a person, God hears everyone's requests, and responds.

Julio expresses thanks every day to the One Who heard his and his wife's prayers. King David wrote in Psalms, "The Lord is close to all who call upon Him in truth." Julio and Sarah, and many other couples like them, have had the privilege of seeing just how true that is.

The Infinitesimal Chance

Before I got married, many women with whom I was friendly wanted to have children eventually, but not until we settled into our careers. By the time we reached our late twenties or early thirties, we felt our biological clocks pounding away as we searched for suitable husbands. When we finally found the men whom we hoped were our lifelong soul-mates, getting pregnant was high on our list of priorities.

For some of us, having babies was easier than for others. One out of six married couples, and one out of five Jewish couples, is unable to have a pregnancy that leads to a live birth within a year of trying. Jewish couples may have a higher rate of infertility because the women tend to be older by the time they try to have children. They often get married later, finish years of higher education, and get established in careers before they start trying to have a baby.

Most singles give little thought to the possibility that they will be infertile. It becomes a preoccupation for many of them after they settle down.

When I got married at the age of thirty-six, I assumed that I would get pregnant almost immediately. After all, my doctor had assured me that I was very fertile, and I wanted very much to start a family. And so, as month after month passed without my getting pregnant, I began to panic. My husband and I started availing ourselves of infertility evaluations and interventions, all to no avail. We spent enormous

Tuning In

amounts of time and energy in doctors' offices, taking blood to laboratories, and going to pharmacies where we got prescriptions filled. Just as we began to sense that something was seriously wrong, despite our doctors saying that we just needed a little bit of assistance, I got pregnant.

We were married more than a year at that point. We were elated that our prayers had finally been answered with a resounding, "Yes, now it's time for you to have a child." No lottery winner could have felt more grateful than we did when we saw the fetal heartbeat on the sonogram. I had had so many sonograms when I wasn't pregnant; it was amazing to finally see a tiny heart beating in the middle of the screen. The minute mass of cells that was the beginning of a little person had started growing a mere six weeks earlier.

Except for daily nausea that lasted from morning until night, nothing marred my day. I was going to have a baby. What could be wrong in the world?

My husband and I looked forward to my next visit to the doctor. How that contrasted with the anxiety we used to feel every time we visited a fertility specialist! Now, instead of worrying what the doctor might find wrong, we were excited about seeing the baby getting bigger and more developed on the sonogram screen.

As I lay back against the examination table, I smiled as I watched the black-and-white picture show on the monitor. There was the little person in waiting. I looked back at the doctor, but he was not smiling. He kept moving the sonogram wand this way and that, but his serious expression never wavered. This was not the jovial obstetrician I knew.

"Is everything okay?" I asked, not expecting to hear anything that didn't confirm that I had a healthy pregnancy.

He grimaced, and poked around for another few seconds. He put down the wand, looked into my eyes, and said, "I'm sorry. There is no longer a heartbeat. The fetus is no longer alive."

I felt a choking ball rise from my chest to my throat. I started to shake, noticing for the first time how chilly it was in the examination room.

Having Children

I was at a loss for words. How could it be that the baby for which I had longed for so many years was dead?! I had never considered the possibility that once alive, the minuscule heart would stop beating.

"Are you sure that the baby is dead?" I asked, wishing that he would change his mind and give me a glimmer of hope.

He nodded. "I wish I had doubts. I know how much you wanted this baby." He paused, and ran his fingers through his straight, dirty-blond hair, pushing it away from his eyes. "Look," he continued, "lots of women miscarry. It's very common. I think the best thing for us to do is to clean you out and have you rest a little bit before trying to get pregnant again. Then, as soon as you are ready, you can try to conceive another time."

I felt a sinking feeling in the pit of my stomach. I glanced over at my husband. He looked like a corpse. I knew that anything that I would say to him would be pointless. He was inconsolable.

As soon as my reproductive system recovered, we began consulting fertility specialists again. They assured us that all was fine, but that more intense assistance would help speed things along. We dutifully sought interventions every month, some of which required us to turn our lives upside down. Twice, we needed to walk four miles each way to a hospital on the Sabbath. Another month, the doctor inserted an assortment of instruments into my reproductive system, left the room, and didn't return for forty-five minutes. No one heard me screaming from where I had been abandoned in the examination room far away from the office. Meanwhile, the doctor forgot that I was there while she made telephone calls, then left for a lunch break. Another month, we were referred to a fertility specialist whose recommendations we faithfully followed. We only found out later that his exorbitant fees were exceeded only by his willingness to subject women to procedures that were known by scientists to be ineffective. Finally, we went to one of the top fertility specialists at a well-known hospital where we were put at the bottom of a year-and-a-half-long waiting list.

Life went on, but my husband and I became obsessed with my reproductive cycles and my infertility. We couldn't make plans without

Tuning In

considering whether or not we would need to be near a hospital on a given day, or whether I would be getting or recovering from a procedure.

One day, I realized that I might be pregnant again. I lost no time running to the pharmacy and getting a home pregnancy test. Miracle of miracles, two red lines showed up in the windows, confirming that a baby was once again growing inside me. It was a year after my miscarriage.

I had now gotten pregnant twice, neither time as a result of infertility interventions. This time I got pregnant during a vacation in Israel, when I least expected it to happen. I attributed it to my endless prayers at the graves of saintly Jews and at the Western Wall. My husband and I were delightfully astounded, and awaited the birth of this child with great anticipation.

A few weeks after we returned to the United States, I was invited to give three lectures at a community Sabbath retreat. My topic after Saturday's lunch was, "Why Bad Things Happen to Good People." One of my patients, who had suffered tremendously, insisted that a good friend of hers come to hear me. The friend was trying to come to terms with a host of tribulations and challenges that she was facing, and my patient assured her that my words would help her find her way. I felt very relaxed and happy to be able to sit with a group of people and talk about normal topics of daily life. For the first time in over a year, I was not preoccupied with being childless.

A few minutes before I was to start speaking, we all said grace after meals. I started to feel cramping, followed by a familiar rush of blood from my body. I couldn't believe this was happening to me again. I felt as if I were being washed away in a torrent that I was helpless to fight. A sensation of drowning overwhelmed me, as part of me was taken away and would never be replaced. My head started spinning. I was so crushed; how could I tell an audience about God being good, that nothing that He does is for a bad purpose, that all suffering in our lives is ultimately constructive? Part of me was screaming in pain. A terrible messenger had come to tell me that I was not the rightful winner of the lottery whose prize I had already mentally banked. It had all been a terrible mistake. It was a dreadful secret that I had to bear in silence, at least for the rest of the afternoon.

I pushed back the tears that wanted to pour forth and gave my talk, with its uplifting message that nothing happens by accident. Everything we undergo is a Divinely engineered circumstance that is tailored to help our soul develop its maximal beauty and connection to its Source. By the time I finished, I knew without a doubt that the new life inside me had died. Meanwhile, my patient's friend came over to tell me how deeply my words had touched her. When the crowd left, I sadly walked back to the rabbi's house where I was staying. In private, I witnessed my body's rejection of the potential life that I had so carefully harbored for those few weeks. I sobbed, feeling physical pain that reflected the emotional torment of my soul. As my heart cried, my intellect told me that God was embracing me, and it was all for an ultimately good purpose.

Three months later, I got a telephone call from the hospital's fertility center. The nurse told me that she had found a way to get me into treatment after a wait of only six, instead of eighteen, months. I jumped at the opportunity. I underwent yet another fertility workup from scratch, my fifth in two years. This time, though, the news was not encouraging. I was nearly thirty-nine-years old, and the tests showed that the end of my fertile years had come. I would have to get monthly blood tests to determine in any given month if I would be fertile that cycle. If my hormone levels were too high for three or four months in a row, there would be no point in subjecting me to any more fertility interventions, as they would not be successful.

Every month we waited with bated breath for the results to come back, and the first two months we were crushed. My hormone levels were so high that they were off the chart, indicating that I could not get pregnant during those cycles. The third month, a miracle occurred. My predictive hormone levels were borderline, and the program accepted me for in-vitro fertilization. I had to inject myself with massive doses of fertility hormones for about a week and get almost daily blood

Tuning In

tests and sonograms. Then, at the ideal time, I would be anesthetized and have my (hopefully fertile) eggs removed so that they could be fertilized and later be re-implanted. For the first time in two years, I had strong hopes that I would actually have a healthy pregnancy. After all, I had referred many friends and patients to the same program. All of them had given birth to healthy children as a result.

I dutifully got my blood drawn the day before the doctor expected to do egg retrieval. My husband and I were looking forward to having dinner that evening with special friends. They had finally had a baby using our hospital's program after twenty-five unsuccessful fertility interventions with another doctor. True to form, we received a terrible phone call that afternoon. It seemed that my blood test showed that my hormones had already surged, and the odds were not good that I would get pregnant if my eggs were retrieved the next day. I understood what the doctor never said — he had botched the timing, and should have done egg retrieval earlier. When pressed, he told me that it would not be unreasonable to continue with the procedure as planned, although the chances of success were smaller. So, I underwent surgery the next day, and a few days later had two embryos implanted. Nearly two weeks later, with every day seeming an eternity, I still was not pregnant.

We endured several more months of torture. Each month, on the appropriate day, I made a three-hour round trip to get my blood drawn and hormone levels tested. Later each day, I was told that my hormone levels were off the chart. Finally, one freezing, windy, January evening, our answering machine broadcast the unlikely news. My numbers were good, they were within normal range, and I should start injecting myself with stimulating hormones that evening.

My husband and I were incredulous, then jubilant. It was Friday night – the Jewish Sabbath. The nearest pharmacy was over a mile away. It was twenty-one degrees outside, with a twenty-mile-an-hour wind. We would have to walk at least half an hour each way to get the drugs that I needed. We couldn't take money or credit cards with us, and we couldn't use the telephone to even find out if the pharmacy had the drugs. What would we do if we got there and the pharmacist

Having Children

said that he didn't have the medication, or that he wouldn't trust us to come back the next day and pay him the $1400 we would owe him for the three boxes of drugs?

Feeling that we had no choice but to hope for the best, we bundled up and set out on our trek. We arrived at the pharmacy, huffing and puffing. We rubbed our stinging, beet-red cheeks, and took off our gloves to massage some warmth into our numb fingers. Luckily, the store was still open. We found the drug dispensary and a very kind-looking, thirty-something man asked if he could help us.

"Do you have any Pergonal in stock tonight?" we asked timidly.

"I always have it in stock," the pharmacist told us. Apparently, there were many other couples in our neighborhood who were going through what we were.

Heaving a sigh of relief, we went on to explain why we had no money with us, and that we would gladly come back the following evening with our credit card in hand. With a disarming smile, he told us not to worry. He would trust us to pay him the next evening. Once again, we were at the top of the emotional roller coaster. This time, we felt as confident as we could that at long last, I would get pregnant.

Everything went along without a hitch during that fertility cycle. When the doctor implanted three embryos in me, they looked very healthy. We all joked about what we would name them. As I rested afterward and recited Psalms, I felt that God was smiling at me, and would finally give me my heart's deepest desire.

Less than two weeks later, my pregnancy test confirmed that I was – miracle of miracles – pregnant. My unrelenting ordeal of the past two-and-a-half years was finally over. I waited, with perverse longing, for the arrival of the familiar all-day morning sickness that I had experienced before.

A few weeks later I was busy writing one of my books, and I felt the sickening rush of blood and cramping that I knew only too well. A scream welled up inside me. I couldn't believe this was happening to me for a third time. Hadn't I suffered enough? "Almighty God," I beseeched, "please make me a miracle and save this child. Please."

Tuning In

I had to wait until the next day to get a sonogram at the hospital where I had conceived. I was bleeding massively, yet the fetus was still alive. I saw the tiny heart beating, a light in the midst of my otherwise dark tunnel. The doctor reassured me that it was possible to still have a healthy pregnancy. He told me that I should go to my local obstetrician for all future care. Although I didn't say it, the cynical part of me wondered if he was sending me away so quickly because he knew that I was likely to miscarry. If I did, the demise of my fetus would mar the success statistics of his fertility program.

When my obstetrician saw the sonogram in his office the next day, he showed me that the fetus was dead.

"It can't be," I challenged him. In an almost condescending way, he showed me what he considered to be definitive proof that the fetus was no longer alive.

"I know that you are a doctor, and I am not, but everything that you showed me was exactly the same way on the sonogram yesterday. I don't believe that the fetus is dead." By that time, I knew far more about reading obstetrical sonograms than I had ever wanted to know.

"Listen," he said nonchalantly, "I'll do a D and C on you as soon as you are ready. The fetus has no heartbeat and the way it's situated there it's obviously not alive. But, if you don't believe me, go across the street and get another sonogram."

I did. Two hours later, my third sonogram in two days showed that I was right. The fetal heart was still beating at a healthy one hundred and forty beats a minute. "Thank you, God," I exclaimed, hoping that this baby's will to live might persevere.

When I turned to look at the radiologist's face, my hopes were dashed very quickly. He was clearly not optimistic.

"Look," he cautioned, "the heartbeat is still good, but you have a huge amount of blood in your uterus." He would say no more about my prognosis.

I continued to bleed massively, and the fetus died a week later.

I had learned to put my feelings in a very special box by this time. If I really got in touch with everything I had been through until then,

Having Children

I would have died with my unborn baby. The part of me that allowed me to survive closed off my heart and doused my tear ducts. I could not allow myself the luxury of feeling my heart break into little pieces, when I had no one to help glue the fragments back together again. I forced myself to detach from what I saw on the sonogram screen, and focused on the future.

"Okay, God," I resolved, "I'm not sure what You want me to do with this. Whatever it is, You're in charge, and I hope that it will affect me so that I can be close to You and do Your will, whatever it is."

It was a close friend's birthday, and I had several friends coming for dinner that night to celebrate. I was hardly in the mood for company and a birthday party. By this time, I had developed the dubious ability to make sure that the show always went on. I didn't want to wallow in my pain, but it certainly wasn't a festive evening for me.

I continued to bleed for the next two months because I didn't want to have any more surgeries, not even another D and C. My body constantly reminded me that it was rejecting the little lives that had been implanted in me. I seemed to be incapable of nurturing or healing.

In the midst of this, a woman whom I had never met called and asked if I would speak to a group of singles at her home. The topic that she had selected was how to find a marriage partner.

"No problem," I agreed. She had gotten my name from a mutual friend at whose home I had spoken the previous year. We worked out the details and I planned to address a group of about fifty people at the beginning of September.

The next night, the same woman (Shulamit) called again. "I don't know anything about you," she admitted, "but there is a rabbi who is coming to my house tomorrow night. He looks at people's ketubot (Jewish wedding contracts) and helps them improve their lives. Would you like to come?"

"When will he see me?" I questioned, wary of consulting any more "miracle men." Unbeknownst to Shulamit, I had already consulted

Tuning In

a host of them in my desperation to have a baby. So far, none of them had provided the magic that I had sought.

"Why don't you come here sometime after midnight?" Shulamit advised.

"Thanks, but no thanks," I retorted. "I have already seen many rabbis. They took my money, told me I should give more charity, gave me amulets, told me to say special prayers for forty days, advised me to eat ruby dust, even insisted that I throw meat to dogs…I have prayed at the burial places of more saintly rabbis than I can count. Nothing ever helped," I told her.

"Look, I don't know you from Adam, and I don't know what you've sought help for," Shulamit pressed, "but this rabbi is really very special. If you can come, I don't think you'll be disappointed."

Feeling that I had nothing left to lose, except for a few more hours of sleep, I went to Shulamit's house after midnight the following evening. I had my rather large Jewish wedding contract with me, but my husband had elected to stay home. He was fed up with consulting people who invariably failed to help us have a child.

Shulamit's living room was filled with people I knew, including the woman who had given her my name. She and her husband were still childless after six years of marriage. He had seen numerous fertility specialists who had all assured him that he could never father a child.

I waited restlessly to see this rabbi. I was too tired to read, and was not in the mood to socialize. Finally, at 1:30 in the morning, his assistant called me into the office. The poor rabbi looked more exhausted than I felt. I didn't have the heart to take up a lot of his time by telling him my tale of woe. I wordlessly put my marriage document in front of him. He pored over it for a few moments.

"Your husband is like a dead man," he said, as he studied the paper further. "It's all because this document wasn't written properly. It needs to be rewritten. Come and see me in three weeks and I will give you a properly written ketubah."

I was dumbfounded. My husband had lost his desire to live since my first miscarriage, and for more than two years he had been profoundly depressed. From the time he saw my first dead fetus' image on the sonogram screen, a part of him had died, too. He wanted more than anything to have a baby with me, and he couldn't understand how a loving and compassionate God had given, then so abruptly taken away. He felt hollow inside. In fact, when we were in the obstetrician's office, and the doctor told us the fetus had died, the doctor was more concerned about my husband's emotional response than mine. The doctor had called the next day to make sure that my husband was OK. He wasn't, but there was little that the doctor or I could do to make things better. I struggled for the next three years to ensure not only my own survival, but that of my husband as well. My husband's physical strength was belied by his emotional vulnerability. Under his muscular veneer was a frail, shattered heart, whose faith in God had eroded. I felt that since he was struggling to survive emotionally and spiritually, I had no one to turn to, except myself and God, during the ordeals that had no end in sight.

When this rabbi zeroed in so quickly on the shell of a person that my husband had become, I felt pained all over again. Finally, I thought I might be talking to someone who could help me end this terrible nightmare.

"How do you know what my husband is like?" I managed.

"It's all here in the ketubah," the rabbi explained. "You see, part of the blessing that comes to a Jewish couple is channeled via their Jewish marriage contract. When it is not written properly, the blessing cannot come. In your case, your husband's father was deceased when you got married. The person who wrote your ketubah wrote your husband's name, son of his father's name, followed by the abbreviation, 'May his memory be for a blessing.' That abbreviation doesn't belong in a wedding document. Whenever it appears in a ketubah, bad things happen to the couple. They have miscarriages, financial problems, and the like. You need your document rewritten and everything will be okay."

As I drove home in the wee hours of the morning, I felt exhausted and cautiously optimistic. I had learned from hard experience that

Tuning In

there are few bona fide mystics in the world today. Prerequisites for being one are that a person is scrupulously observant and a Torah scholar, and few such mystics make themselves known to the public. People today are desperate to find miracle workers who, through magical means, can give us what we want. I had already met my share of those who were adept at giving blessings and separating those they blessed from their money. I had met only a few who had truly helped others. Had God put this rabbi in my path as a conduit for bringing greater holiness into my life, or to test whether I would stop hoping for intermediaries like rabbis and doctors to provide me with the child that I so urgently wanted? I decided to pray that I had undergone whatever personal changes I needed to make, and that changing the ketubah would allow me to be the person that God deemed ready to receive a child.

Convincing my husband to get a new ketubah was another matter altogether. Not only had he given up hope that we would have a baby, he had given up hope that we would even be able to adopt. We had already explored several options for adoption and none had panned out. My husband was certainly not receptive to the idea that changing a ketubah could alter the spiritual reality of our lives.

Finally, my husband offered the following compromise: he was going to be on call the Sunday that we were supposed to get the new ketubah. If he got called into the hospital, he would assume that God did not want us to get a new marriage document. If he wasn't called in, he would join me.

Three weeks later, I was very relieved when my husband showed up at the rabbi's apartment. The rabbi gave my husband the new ketubah and my husband gave it to me in front of two valid Jewish witnesses. As I held the document, the rabbi said, "Please God, you should have a baby within a year." I hoped that his prayer would go to the Almighty and be responded to in the way that I wished. On the other hand, it was hard to imagine that after so much yearning and praying that my dream would come true. At the time, I was still bleeding from my third miscarriage.

Having Children

The next month, my body finally returned to normal, and I called the fertility doctor. "Should I come in for blood tests this month?" I asked.

In an avuncular voice he responded, "Don't bother. You've already spent almost three years and over $50,000 trying to have a baby, and nothing has worked. We know why you keep having miscarriages or don't get pregnant in the first place. You have no good eggs left. Some women reach menopause earlier, some later. You are no longer fertile. If you still want to have a baby, either adopt or go to a donor egg program. Your chances of ever having a healthy pregnancy are infinitesimal."

I was crushed, yet I agreed that it was futile for me to go back to the hospital. On the other hand, I believed that God wanted me to have a child. How He would make it happen, I had no idea.

Two weeks later, my husband and I visited Israel for the Jewish holidays. We stayed in Jerusalem, prayed a lot at the Western Wall, and absorbed the holiness of the land. Two weeks after we came back to the United States, I discovered that I was pregnant for the fourth time. As weeks turned into months, and the pregnancy advanced uneventfully, it seemed that we might finally have the baby that we so desired.

Our daughter was born a month premature. I gave birth on a Friday night, the first day of summer. It was ten months after the rabbi changed our ketubah and prayed that I should have a baby within the year.

When I saw this tiny creation for the first time, I was not prepared for what a newborn baby looks like. I had expected a Gerber baby. My child looked like a combination of Popeye and a cone head, covered with mayonnaise and ketchup.

"Isn't she the most beautiful thing you've ever seen?" my husband gushed, his eyes blinded by love. Indeed, when I saw her after she was cleaned up a few hours later, she was the most beautiful thing that I had ever seen.

Tuning In

A few months later, the rabbi visited our town, and I brought my baby to see him. "This is the baby that you told us we were going to have," I reported.

He looked at her, smiled, and then looked at me. "You're going to have another one," he said confidently.

I nearly fell off my chair. I was already forty years old, and the doctors had told me that I couldn't even have the baby that was cradled in my arms. I was going to have another one?! I was too stunned to reply.

My husband asked, "When?"

"Soon," the rabbi smiled.

Over the next six months, my husband urged me to stop nursing our baby so that I would have at least a remote chance of getting pregnant again. I spoke to two world-renowned fertility specialists and they both agreed that in the best of circumstances, nursing would drastically reduce the possibility of a fertile woman's conceiving. In my case, they assured me that there was no chance that I could get pregnant nursing every few hours around the clock. I finally compromised with my husband: I would stop nursing when our baby was a year old if I still had not conceived.

Twice every day, I prayed that I should get pregnant again and not have to stop nursing. When our daughter was eleven months old, she, my husband and I went to Australia. I gave a series of talks there, and we also planned to tour and go scuba diving on the Great Barrier Reef.

When our daughter was one week shy of a year, my husband told me, "Look, our daughter will be over a year old by the time we get back to the United States. You need to start getting used to the idea that you will need to wean her." Our baby was happily nursing about eight times a day at the time. I said nothing to my husband. I just intensified my prayers to get pregnant.

Three days later, on the eve of Shavuot (the holiday that commemorates God's giving the Torah to the Jewish people), I discovered that I was pregnant. My husband could not believe, under the circumstances of nursing so much, being over forty, and being told

Having Children

by two world-class fertility specialists that I could not get pregnant, that I was not mistaken. I had to show him the pregnancy test stick to convince him that it was not wishful thinking on my part.

I gave birth to our second child the following winter.

Part IV:
What Goes Around, Comes Around

What Goes Around, Comes Around

Reaping What We Sow

Sheila was a bright, energetic, likeable young woman. She was eager to work for a company that would give her lots of responsibility with a salary to match. She was ecstatic when she was hired for a managerial position with a computer software company. Unfortunately, she did not realize at the time that many people in the company had agendas that had nothing to do with productivity and creativity. In fact, some of her closest associates were petty, jealous, and felt threatened by a woman in such a powerful and lucrative position.

Six months after she started her new job, she got a promotion and a raise. She was deliriously happy, did stellar work, and proceeded to develop marketing strategies that were reflected by higher earnings for the company.

Once Sheila was established in her new position, her boss, Larry, had plans for her. He decided to delegate to her some of his unpleasant tasks. The first of these was to fire a salesman, Marco, that Larry had disliked intensely for years, but for political reasons had wanted someone else to fire.

Sheila and Larry had meetings several times a month from the time that she started working at the company. Although he was short, he cut an impressive image with his perfectly coiffed salt-and-pepper hair, which faded to totally gray at the temples, his Oscar de la Renta glasses, his Christian Dior shirts, Gucci belts, and $600 suits. He

Tuning In

had Mediterranean good looks, and his impeccable grooming and exquisite taste gave him an unmistakable presence. His avuncular and solicitous style with her led her to trust him as a mentor and as a friend. If he wanted to get rid of anyone in the company, she assumed that he must have a good reason for wanting to do so.

Marco worked for the company only two days a week and did private consulting work the other three days. He had already been with the company for nine years and was their most senior salesperson. Sheila had seen the wedding pictures of both Larry and Marco that they respectively displayed in their offices. She thought that it was ironic that both men bore a striking resemblance to one another, based on their pictures from their late twenties. During the next twenty years, though, Larry had cultivated a different image for himself and grew into a polished, charismatic leader. Marco seemed a caricature of Woody Allen, albeit with Italian-American roots.

Sheila did not particularly like Marco. He had an ego the size of a football field and earned the highest hourly salary among the salespeople, although his commissions were the least impressive. He knew the business inside and out, but he occasionally harassed the females that he was assigned to train. They, in turn, bitterly complained to Sheila, who fumed to the trainees about his chauvinistic behavior. However, she never directly confronted Marco about his unpleasant behavior – she only talked about him to others behind his back.

When Larry asked her to fire Marco, Sheila was only too happy to oblige. Larry found Marco's personality very irritating, although truth be told, Sheila wondered if what really bothered Larry was the fact that Marco reminded Larry of his own humble roots. While Larry complained about the fact that Marco got a much higher salary than the other salespeople, Sheila had the suspicion that Larry felt somehow competitive with his subordinate. Nonetheless, Sheila was only too happy, as often happens in such places, to assassinate Marco's character when Larry disparaged Marco. It made Sheila feel as if she were part of a special club that did not share these flaws, but was far above them.

What Goes Around, Comes Around

Sheila divulged derogatory information to Larry that further sealed Marco's fate. Larry instructed Sheila about how to fire people in general, and Marco in particular. It all had to be done according to protocol. One couldn't simply fire another employee because he or she got under one's skin, although that was often the true reason underlying many corporate terminations. Sheila was soon to learn that politics, much more than lack of ability, was the main reason that people got axed.

The following week, Sheila reviewed the plan for Marco's termination with Larry. First, she would confront Marco with complaints from his trainees and tell him to cease and desist from his intrusive behavior. Second, she would insist that he stop leaving work fifteen minutes early every day, as he had done for years. Third, he would be required to meet with the trainees the full two hours that was mandated every week instead of his usual hour and a half. Fourth, he would no longer have the right to refuse to work with the least gratifying customers, as he had done as a matter of course. Marco had made it clear that there were only certain clients with whom he would work, supposedly because his sales techniques would only be productive with them. Sheila told him that if he turned down any client that was assigned to him for any reason, it would be immediate grounds for his dismissal. Sheila made sure to commit every point to writing and handed him a copy so that he would have no legal grounds for complaint later.

When Sheila met with Marco, she was surprised at his reaction to being told that he was on probation. He acted like a chastened dog, apologized profusely, and promised to redress every problem ASAP. He made it clear to Sheila that keeping his job was very important to him. He had one son in private high school and another in a pricey college. He needed this job to afford their tuition. At his age, forty-nine, and during the uncertain business climate of that time, finding another sales job would not be easy.

Sheila could not imagine why the salary that he made for his part-time work was so important to him. After all, it was but a fraction of

Tuning In

either son's tuition. He probably made five times more money every day as a consultant than he made spending the same amount of time selling.

Three months passed. The trainees had stopped complaining about Marco's behavior. He worked the hours that he was supposed to work. He didn't even grumble when he was assigned two clients that no one else could stand working with. He offered to give a seminar to the novice salespeople on some new software programs that he was selling.

A few days later, Sheila met with Larry to review a number of work matters. One of the first items on Larry's agenda was Marco.

"So, how's the jerk doing now?" Larry inquired with rancor in his voice.

Sheila looked at him quizzically. What jerk did he have in mind?

"You know, Marco," Larry answered impatiently. "Has the jerk gotten his act together?"

Sheila was taken aback. Larry was usually soft-spoken, avuncular, polite and even solicitous of her. She had never seen him express such hostility to any employee. She glanced at his eyes and saw a rage behind them that was frightening.

"Well, actually, he has," Sheila hesitantly replied. "I went over the list of problems as you and I had discussed, and I would say that he's corrected ninety percent of them."

"I don't care," Larry growled through his polished smile and capped front teeth. "Find a way to fire him. He reminds me of Jerry Lewis. He discredits the human race. I don't like him and I don't want to see him around here any more."

For the first time, Sheila understood much more about Larry than she ever wanted to know.

"Do I make myself clear?" Larry asked with a cold, controlled venom that he injected when necessary. The force of his soft-spoken words dispelled any doubts that Sheila still harbored about firing Marco.

"But what do I do with the fact that he's corrected ninety percent of the issues that I raised with him?" Sheila countered.

What Goes Around, Comes Around

"Use the remaining ten percent," Larry insisted, "and do what you have to do. Now, let's go over the proposal that you put together for Wednesday's meeting." Sheila understood that the issue with Marco was now closed.

The next day, Sheila called Marco into her office. "It's time to review your probation," she recommended with forced pleasantness. "Please sit down."

Marco seated himself opposite Sheila at her desk. His dark brown eyes and neutral expression signaled that he expectantly waited for a reprieve from his sentence. It was not forthcoming.

"I'm sorry, Marco," Sheila began with a projected air of confidence, "but we won't be able to continue keeping you on staff. We're having budgetary problems and your sales performance has been on the low end for years. We're going to have to let you go."

Marco was crestfallen. He struggled to fight back tears. "Couldn't you please find a way to keep me here? I need the income. I'll take a salary cut. You can ask me to do anything. Please, whatever you do, just don't fire me."

Sheila had already absorbed some of Larry's sang-froid. Marco's request almost struck her as pathetic instead of arousing sympathy. "I'm sorry, Marco, I can't. You'll be on salary until the end of the month. In the meantime, you might want to go to the personnel office to find out what benefits you are entitled to get after you leave."

Marco sat frozen in his seat, dazed and expressionless. He looked as if someone had just informed him that his wife had died.

Sheila did not want him to grieve in her office. "Marco," Sheila gently urged, "you need to go back to your office. I have a client waiting." She opened the door, then added, "I'm sorry," as he trudged past her, his head hanging down. He barely managed to put one foot in front of the other.

As she closed the door, she quickly pushed aside her fleeting doubts that she shouldn't have fired Marco. Perhaps she could have made a stronger case to Larry about why he should stay on staff. After all, Larry was a powerful man. Why hadn't he fired Marco years ago?

Tuning In

Was he such a coward that he could only rely on her to do this odious task?

Perhaps she should stop entertaining such possibilities, she quickly admonished herself. She felt relieved that Marco would no longer be around. She had internalized enough of Larry's attitudes that she quickly focused only on Marco's demerits and on none of his good points. She vilified him in her efforts to assuage her guilt, and then tried a different tactic when that didn't work. She would make him a going-away party and ask the other employees to contribute a nice gift.

A few months after Marco's departure, Sheila began to notice that every time there were company managerial meetings, the managers began bashing whichever manager was not there. One of them was always on vacation or out-of-town on business. The initial feeling that she had gotten at the corporation was that it was one big family. Now she was seeing that the family had all sorts of rivalries. The members vied for the boss's attention, were jealous of one another, and seemed to delight in toppling one another when backstabbing opportunities arose.

Sheila had to admit to herself that she enjoyed partaking in these ganging-up forays. It reminded her of the adolescent carping and backbiting that she and her friends had indulged in as sophomores in high school. They raised character assassination to a high art form. She, and the other managers, actually savored the thrill they felt making themselves feel important at someone else's expense – especially when that someone wasn't there to defend himself.

Six months later, Sheila realized with no small amount of trepidation that the honeymoon that she had enjoyed with the company had worn off. Worse, she was going on vacation in a month. What would the other managers say about her during her three weeks away? She considered canceling her trip in order to make sure that no one did to her what she and her colleagues had been doing to the rest of the group for nearly a year.

What Goes Around, Comes Around

Ah, well, she decided, you can't avoid being criticized forever. You're not perfect, but neither is anyone else. After many sleepless nights, and daily flashes of anxiety, she decided to take her vacation as planned. Yet, throughout her entire trip, something gnawed at her. She woke up every morning with a pain in the pit of her stomach, and unpleasant thoughts intruded into her mind throughout the day. At night, when no diversions distracted her, she shuddered with anxiety as she lay in bed trying to fall asleep.

It turned out that Sheila's premonitions were well-founded. A few days after she came back to work, she noticed an ominous, tense feeling in the air. Larry scheduled an appointment with her for the end of the week, and she sensed a curtness in his voice that had never been there before when he spoke to her.

As soon as she entered his office, he motioned her to sit down. He didn't waste any time getting to the heart of the matter.

"You know, Sheila, your work here has been deteriorating for some time. You haven't developed any innovative ideas for almost a year. Your staff doesn't like the way you manage them. Your client load has gone down by ten percent. The other managers have logged numerous complaints about you."

Sheila felt as if he had assaulted her with a machine gun. She barely registered one complaint in her mind before he rapid-fired the next. It took her a few moments to regain her composure and to formulate a credible response.

"I'm really not sure what kind of work deterioration you're referring to, or what kind of managers' complaints you've received. No one has said a word to me about any dissatisfaction."

Wordlessly, Larry produced a folder filled with pages of company stationery and showed her a few complaint letters from her staff. A sick feeling rose in Sheila's stomach. The complaints were about facts that were true, but the reasons explaining those facts were completely distorted. For example, her group did not meet their sales quota one month and Larry attributed that to her poor managerial capabilities. Actually, her best salesperson had been in a car accident and needed to be in a rehabilitation hospital that month. How could Larry blame that problem on her?

Another complaint was from one of her supervisors. He maintained that she was conducting private business during company hours. It was true that she spent two hours a week consulting privately with a different company, but her supervisor had asked her to do this! Her supervisor thought that by creating this relationship, Sheila would ultimately gain his confidence and he would become a major client of their company. Besides, she always worked an extra two hours every week to make up for that lost time.

Larry had constructed a list of complaints that reminded her of the man who was asked, "So when did you stop beating your wife?" No matter how hard and how well she defended herself, she made no noticeable dent in Larry's negative opinion of her. She realized that her days at the company were numbered. By the time their meeting ended, Larry put her on probation for three months as a mere formality. It was clear that there was nothing she could do to salvage her position. Larry ushered her to the door, as she tried to rise against the weight of the iron ball in her heart. Dizzy with anxiety, she trudged back to her office.

With her head spinning, and her world having fallen down around her, Sheila asked herself why God was making this happen to her. An image immediately danced into her head. Marco's face appeared in front of her, looking as if he had been stabbed. The parallels between his situation and hers were patently obvious. Both of them had had good and bad points, strengths and shortcomings. She had focused only on his shortcomings and so the same was done to her. She desperately wanted her job, just as he had wanted his job. Larry was as callous to her as she had been to Marco. No explanations that she gave were satisfactory. Larry managed to twist everything that she said to make her look like a fool. Similarly, she had not been interested in any of Marco's explanations of others' complaints against him. She had assassinated his character to others and now she knew what it felt like to have the same done to her.

What Goes Around, Comes Around

She let herself wallow in her misery and despair for a few moments, then went next door. Don, one of the salespeople, was sitting in his office, writing some notes. She knocked and asked if she could disturb him for a few minutes. He peered above his reading glasses and nodded.

"Why did you write Larry a letter complaining about me without ever discussing your criticisms with me first?" she asked in a mildly rebuking voice.

Don wasn't perturbed by her brazenness, nor by the revelation of his private character assassination of her. "Larry told me that either I write criticisms of you, or I would lose my job," he responded matter-of-factly.

Sheila couldn't believe her ears. That is exactly the reason why she had fired Marco. Larry had told her to do it! She was being punished in exactly the way that Judaism teaches that life responds to us – measure for measure. What we do to others, and the ways that we sin, come back to haunt and hurt us in exactly the same ways that we misbehaved in the first place.

The next week, Sheila walked out of a meeting and ran into one of the other managers. She had never particularly liked Jonny, but she had gone out of her way over the years to help him achieve his work objectives. She had advised him, listened to him, and given him lots of emotional support when he was bewildered as to how to deal with people in the business.

"Hi, Sheila," Jonny called in a friendly voice. "Say, I'm really sorry about what happened to you. I didn't want to say such terrible things about you, but what could I do? My job was on the line. Larry told me that he would fire me if I didn't find things to criticize about you."

Sheila was shocked. She hadn't known that Jonny was one of the people who had caused her downfall. What an ingrate! She was so furious with him that she simply turned away and left.

Back at her office, she decided to visit two more people before the end of the day. One was a supervisor whose complaint she had seen in Larry's office. He had accused her of doing private business during office time after telling her to do private consulting there. The other was the office manager who had also lodged a formal complaint.

First, she went to Dick's office. When Dick was hired, Sheila had helped him learn the ropes during his first six months with the company. Unfortunately, Dick had never done an adequate job because he was in the process of getting divorced. He spent almost all day, every day, on the phone speaking to his lawyer, accountant, and therapist.

Dick was just finishing one of his countless personal phone calls when Sheila knocked on his door. "Dick, I just want you to know that I saw the letter that you wrote against me, and most of the accusations that you made against me weren't even true. The others were distorted. If you had complaints about me, why didn't you ever discuss them with me?"

"Oh, I didn't think that anyone would take my complaints seriously," Dick replied nonchalantly. "I figured that if anyone thought that my complaints had merit, they would investigate them themselves. I knew that they were only hearsay. I never meant for them to be viewed as facts."

Sheila was so disgusted, she left the room without comment.

Last, she went to Tina, the office manager. Tina was from a lower socio-economic background. She had barely squeezed through high school and was a secretary when Sheila had joined the company. Tina had teased, bleached blond hair that flowed over her shoulders. The gum that she chewed often cracked while she chomped away. She wore heavy makeup, low-cut blouses and high-heeled shoes that were much more suitable for disco dancing in smoky rooms with ear-shattering music than they were for doing corporate work.

Shortly after Sheila's arrival at the company, Larry had asked her what she thought of the "teeny-bopper" who worked for her and for several other managers. Sheila understood that her response would mean continued employment or termination for Tina. Although she thought that Tina's appearance was out-of-line for a corporate setting,

What Goes Around, Comes Around

Sheila appreciated that Tina usually worked hard and tried to please the people whose work she typed.

Sheila had told Larry, "Tina is a pretty conscientious worker. I think that she has room to grow, and I think that in a few years' time she'll be capable of taking on a lot more responsibility."

Two years later, Sheila had recommended to Larry that Tina be promoted to office manager when the prior office manager left the company. Larry promoted Tina based on Sheila's advice. By that time, Tina filled the role quite nicely. Tina never knew that it was Sheila's doing that got her promoted.

Now, Sheila approached Tina and asked, "Do you think that any of the office staff has complaints about me?"

Tina stared at her. "You must be kidding," Tina responded with contempt in her voice. "I don't think that any one of us can think of anything nice to say about you."

Once again, Sheila involuntarily froze when she heard Tina's words echo in Sheila's ears. "NO ONE CAN THINK OF ANYTHING NICE TO SAY ABOUT YOU." How many times had Sheila been unwilling, or unable, to find anything nice to say about Marco, or about the other managers whom she had spent many meetings assassinating?

Sheila returned to her office, depressed. At the same time, she was struck by how matters had come full-circle since the time that she had put Marco on probation.

By the time her probation was over, it didn't matter to Larry that Sheila had given a stellar performance for three months. He treated her the same way that she had treated Marco some time before. Larry invented several creative pretexts to force her to leave ignominiously.

Duly chastened, Sheila resolved never again to be so cavalier about saying bad things about others, or about casting aspersions on people in ways that jeopardized their livelihood. She was troubled for a long time about losing her job in such a humiliating way.

A few weeks later, Sheila telephoned a friend one night and shared her tale of woe with Adrian. Adrian was in her sixties and had become

Tuning In

very wise due to her life experiences. Adrian listened attentively to Sheila's story, then responded in a caring and warm voice.

"Sheila, I've been around a lot. When I was young, I used to be upset by all of the injustice in the world. As I grew older, I started to notice that what goes around, comes around. Just wait, you'll see. Everyone eventually gets exactly what is coming to them."

In due time, Sheila found a job that was much more suitable for her. It paid more than her previous job, made good use of her abilities, and had a pleasant atmosphere. It was also devoid of the malicious backstabbing and nasty politics that had played such a role in her prior employment.

A few months later, Sheila realized that some mail was mistakenly sent to her at her former workplace. She called the office to see if it could be forwarded to her home. When the secretary, Ellen, answered the phone, Sheila exchanged pleasantries with her.

"So, how is life at your company?" Sheila pleasantly inquired.

"Oh, you haven't heard?" Ellen inquired. "A lot has changed since you left. A month after you left, Larry fired Jonny. Jonny's going to have a terrible time finding a job anywhere else."

Sheila was thunderstruck. Jonny had thought that he would hold onto his job by making her lose hers. He had gotten punished measure for measure! He made her lose her job and then he lost his! In addition, the one who fired Jonny was the same boss that Jonny had thought would take care of him if Jonny only acted unethically.

Sheila was about to interject her question about forwarding mail when Ellen continued, "And that's not all. Dick was diagnosed with a curable form of cancer last month and Larry fired him, too. Dick will be okay, but he's out of a job for at least a few months while he gets treatment. And by the way, how are you doing?"

Sheila thought about how fortunate she was on two counts: One, she had her good health, a great job, and best of all, her integrity. Two, she had seen a Divine Hand reveal itself by meting out punishment measure for measure. It was very comforting to know that events in her life were neither haphazard nor unjust. She felt that she had

What Goes Around, Comes Around

been given a tremendous gift of being able to see how Divine eyes continually watched everything that she, and those around her, did.

What a blessing to be reprimanded when we misbehave, then be guided as to how to improve ourselves soon afterward!

"I'm doing really well, thank you," Sheila replied sincerely. "Things couldn't be better."

A War Story

In June 1973, Arabs from the countries surrounding Israel were heavily armed as they prepared to destroy the Jewish people. The avowed goal of her Arab neighbors was to drive Israeli Jews into the sea. The Arabs attacked on the holiest day of the Jewish calendar, Yom Kippur, when Jews all over Israel were in synagogue, repenting and fasting. With lightning speed, soldiers traveled to the fronts, and doctors were called into hospitals to tend to the massive numbers of casualties. At Soroka Hospital in Beersheva, sixty casualties at a time were flown in from the war front in the Sinai desert. Most of these young men were in their late teens and twenties. They were brought into the emergency room where doctors worked around the clock, mending their torn and tattered bodies. As soon as the last of the group received care, the next load of sixty casualties arrived.

Due to the dire need for doctors on the fronts and in the hospitals, even medical students were pressed into service as medics. Medics were often the first ones to tend to the wounded on the battlefields. At one point, a veteran doctor in the field, Arnon Avigdor, was hit in the chest by shrapnel as a shell destroyed his tank. As Avigdor lay severely injured and bleeding, Mordechai Segall, a medical student, lost no time administering aid. He dressed the wound, inserted a tube into Avigdor's chest to drain the site, and did everything necessary to keep Avigdor alive. Due to the battle that was raging, it was impossible for a helicopter to quickly evacuate Avigdor and the other wounded. There was simply no place it could land.

Tuning In

Meanwhile, Avigdor went in and out of consciousness. If he did not get to a hospital quickly, he would die. Although other wounded men also needed help, Segall insisted that Avigdor was too precious to lose, and he stayed by Avigdor's side monitoring his vital signs and keeping him alive. Forty-five minutes later, a helicopter finally arrived, and managed to evacuate Avigdor and other wounded to the hospital. When Segall last saw Avigdor, his ministering efforts had paid off. He knew that Avigdor would live.

After the war, Segall finished his long years of study as a medical student and decided to become a surgeon. He did his residency at a busy hospital in Jerusalem. At the end of his residency, he registered to take his licensing boards in surgery. When the day of the exams arrived, Segall entered the room where a group of expert surgeons were waiting to test him. One of the doctors stepped away from the others and walked over to Segall. Segall felt a surge of anxiety and could not imagine what he had done to warrant this break in protocol.

"Dr. Mordechai Segall?" the surgeon asked.

Segall nodded.

"Congratulations. You already passed."

The doctor congratulating him was Arnon Avigdor, the man whose life he had saved five years before.

What Goes Around, Comes Around

Auschwitz and Antibiotics

I was very annoyed. I had been waiting for the van to take me to the Tel Aviv Airport since 8:45 P.M. It was now 9:20, and my transportation was nowhere in sight. When the driver finally pulled up ten minutes later, he never apologized for his extreme lateness. All he said was, "Are you waiting for me? Yes? Get in."

I get very disturbed when people don't respect my time. Time is one of the most precious gifts we have, and I hate wasting it. But tonight, I was especially perturbed at the driver's casualness about making me wait unnecessarily. I had wanted to tell my daughters their bedtime stories and hug them for a few extra minutes before leaving them for several days to attend my father's funeral.

Before I left the house, my four-year-old had implored, "Mommy, can you leave me a note so that I don't miss you so much while you're gone?"

"Leave one for me, too," the six-year-old pleaded.

And so, I left each a love note before I left. Each promised to keep hers under her pillow until I returned. As I was about to step out the door, my older daughter called, "Mommy. Here. Take this with you so that you'll have something to remember me by and won't miss me so much." With that, she handed me one of her favorite marbles.

Tuning In

"I love you," they both chimed together, as we hugged for the last time. I raced to the street to catch what I thought would be the waiting van.

Instead of fuming at the driver's inconsideration, I decided to focus on the gift of my children's love. It was but a few days before the Jewish New Year, and I had resolved to work very hard this year to love other Jews. Loving in the abstract was easy. When people were annoying or inconsiderate, it was much more of a challenge. That night, I felt as if I were getting a graduate seminar in the topic.

Not only didn't the driver apologize for not calling me to let me know that he was going to make six stops before picking me up, he still had more stops to make! I needed to be at the airport at 10:00 P.M. to buy a ticket for my flight that evening. Meanwhile, the airport was an hour away if one drove there directly. To make matters worse, our driver was in no hurry to get us anywhere.

The next passenger we picked up was visibly incensed at having been told to be outside at 8:45. "Why did you make me wait for forty-five minutes?" he yelled.

The driver calmly replied, "If you get so nervous about such small things, you'll need to see a doctor."

The man yelled back, "I am a doctor! I work at Shaarei Tzedek Hospital!"

The Breslover Hasid sitting in front of the doctor was on his way to Uman in Eastern Europe. He was planning to visit the grave of the holy Rabbi Nachman. His curiosity piqued, the Breslover asked, "What kind of doctor are you?"

Within five minutes, the nine former strangers in the van were playing Jewish geography and getting to know each other. The doctor had come from Klausenburg and was returning to Romania for a reunion of childhood friends. When I asked him if he had known the Klausenburger Rebbe, a saintly man, the doctor nodded.

"When the Rebbe lived in Israel, I used to go to his Passover seders some years."

What Goes Around, Comes Around

The Klausenburger Rebbe had lived in Europe with his wife and eleven children during World War II. The Rebbe's children and wife were all murdered by the Nazis and died sanctifying God's Name.

After the war, the Rebbe found himself in a Displaced Persons camp. One day, he saw a young Jewish woman wandering bare legged in the camp. The Rebbe kindly approached her and asked why she wasn't wearing stockings. "I don't own anything in the world except for the clothes that I'm wearing," the teenager responded. The Rebbe had pity on her and removed his own socks and gave them to the girl.

When the Rebbe came to Israel, he founded Laniado Hospital, not far from Tel Aviv. He wanted it to be a place that was run according to Jewish law, with pure loving-kindness as an integral component of the medical services performed there. The Rebbe reasoned that the Nazis had acted out of pure hatred; the remedy would be a place where pure love would be meted out in abundance.

In addition to founding this amazing hospital, the Rebbe always felt a strong sense of allegiance to other survivors of the Holocaust. He knew what it felt like to be bereft of his family, his community, and his entire way of life. So the Rebbe invited countless other survivors to his Sabbath meals and to his Passover seder (special ritual supper) the first night of Passover.

"What were his seders like?" I asked the doctor.

"I cannot describe it," he replied. "They were so full of joy and happiness and people celebrating life."

Just then, my cell phone rang.

"Lisa, this is Jeff. Dad just passed away."

When I heard the words, I felt as if someone had just pierced me through. In an instant, the breath went out of me and I felt totally spent. I had been sitting on pins and needles for days, both hoping for, and dreading, the painful moment that I knew would inevitably arrive. Just a month earlier, I had watched helplessly as my father struggled many times to get out of bed. His face would contort with pain as his aide tried to ease him, despite his contracted muscles, into a wheelchair. His anemic blood was not oxygenating his brain enough to

Tuning In

keep him oriented. He was often frightened by the lack of continuity, predictability and order in his life. My attempts to reassure him were appreciated but short-lived. He was easily fatigued during my visits, and usually needed to make painful efforts to be placed, after increasingly shorter intervals, back in bed.

I had admired my father's heroic battles against his infirmities during the ups and downs of seven, often emotionally draining, years. It had become increasingly clear to all of us that, as he summoned all of his weakening strength to less and less effect during the prior months, he could no longer prevail against his mortality. While I certainly wished that he would not leave this world, I also realized that he was paying an intense price to stay. By the time my brother told me that my father's struggle had ended, I was relieved that he was finally at peace.

I said the blessing acknowledging that God is the true Judge, spoken when one learns of someone's death. It was the last prayer that, as someone awaiting the burial of a close relative, I would be allowed to recite until after my father was interred.

I responded to my brother, "I'm on my way to the airport now. I'll be in Baltimore by 9:30 tomorrow morning. When will the funeral be?"

"I'm not sure. I'll have to let you know," he answered, his voice breaking with emotion.

As soon as I ended the conversation, the other passengers extended their condolences. I asked the man in front of me, the second Breslover Hasid in the van, what he did for a living.

"I study full-time in a yeshiva," he replied.

I had searched for a book called *Mourning in Halacha* (halacha means Jewish law) before I left home. When a close relative passes away, Judaism prescribes many rituals for the bereaved that are designed to help them grieve properly and give respect and spiritual merit to the deceased. The book, which I had owned for years, was nowhere to be found when I needed it. As I left my house for the airport, I had wondered how I would find out all of the things that I was supposed

What Goes Around, Comes Around

to do, or not do, between the time my father passed away and the time that my family would sit *shiva* (observe a week of mourning).

Divine providence began to shine through the darkness. The Hasid in front of me had lost his father the year before, and he knew all about the appropriate customs and rituals. When I asked him if he could summarize them to me, he was only too happy to oblige. We reached the airport just as he concluded his synopsis.

"You know," he said as we exited the van, "it is a very great honor to the deceased for people to study the Oral Law in his memory. Take my phone number. Call me when you get back, and I will help you arrange for people to learn in his memory."

As he gave me his phone number, the other Hasid approached me. His dark eyes peered into mine with empathy as he said, "May God comfort you from your pain and only send you happy events during the coming year."

What had begun as an annoying incident with a rude taxi driver had ended by revealing tremendous Divine and human compassion. I had been unable to find my book on mourning, and God had arranged matters so that another passenger in the van had told me exactly what I needed to know. At a time when I had no one familiar to comfort me, He arranged sympathetic strangers to do the job. My experience reminded me that no matter how much Jews fight with one another, we are still one big family that depends on, and helps, each other in times of adversity. I was going to see that idea played out repeatedly over the next few hours and days as strangers showered me with love.

When I arrived at the El Al counter to arrange my seat assignment, the computer had already recorded the reason for my buying a ticket at the last minute. The agent smiled, "I put you in a seat next to an empty seat. I'm closing that seat so that you'll have some room. I'd like to make things as comfortable as possible for you. Have a nice flight."

A little kindness from strangers goes a long way, especially at such difficult times. And what goes around, comes around.

Seventeen hours later, I arrived at Kennedy airport in New York. I was exhausted. I trudged down to the domestic gate for my connecting

Tuning In

flight from Kennedy to Baltimore-Washington International. I felt very edgy. Not only did I feel the limbo and fatigue of being in transit, I began to feel uncomfortable having the status of an *onen*. An onen is someone whose close relative (parent, sibling, child, or spouse) has died but has not yet been buried. Due to their presumed preoccupation with funeral arrangements and the like, an onen may not pray, say blessings, or study Torah. Normally, I would have spent my waiting time saying morning prayers and reading a book on some type of Torah matter. Instead, I sat in the empty terminal waiting for the time to pass. When I ate or drank, I couldn't even recite a blessing as I normally would have, thanking God for His bounty.

I used the bathroom. When I exited, it felt unnatural not to recite the customary blessing expressing my appreciation for the fact that, unlike my recently departed father, my kidneys were working perfectly. I sat down restlessly on one of the hundreds of empty seats and noted the time. It was 6:10 in the morning. I had almost two hours to wait before I could board my connecting flight.

I downed a handful of crackers, and then reflexively felt bad that I was taking undeserved sustenance from God without even a simple acknowledgment. At that moment, I appreciated something that I had never appreciated before. Jewish tradition teaches that the greatest gift that God gives us is the ability to earn His gifts, rather than feeling like welfare recipients who get them without any effort on our parts. One way that we earn our daily sustenance is to acknowledge its Source, then use the nourishment we receive to sustain us so that we can spiritually perfect God's world. It felt very bad to simply take with no opportunity to give back.

As I pondered this, an old lady whom I had seen on my El Al flight slowly walked in my direction. "Do you know how much it costs to call Baltimore from the pay phones?" she inquired.

I knew exactly. "It costs one dollar for four minutes. Do you have change?" I asked her.

What Goes Around, Comes Around

She carefully unwrapped a small plastic bag, filled with coins of every description. There was a twenty-franc piece, some British pence, Canadian dimes, Austrian kroner…but no American money.

"Here, take my phone card," I offered.

"I want to pay you back," she insisted.

"Please don't," I demurred. "If you want to give a few coins to the charity of your choice when you get to your daughter's house, that would be fine."

This nameless stranger slowly ambled over to the bank of phones and apprised her daughter of her imminent arrival.

When she came back, she sat two seats away. I tried to size her up. She appeared to be in her late seventies, and looked frail and petite. She could not have been more than five feet tall, even wearing heeled shoes. She wore a brunette wig, covered by an unattractive scarf, the kind a babushka might wear. That told me that she was probably Hasidic, from Eastern Europe. Her face was etched with wrinkles, although her deep, brown eyes were filled with energy and vigor. She spoke with a strange accent that I couldn't place. She sounded French, Hungarian and Israeli, all mixed together. My father, I reminisced, was pretty good at identifying where people were from based on their accents. I inherited some of that ability, but in her case, I was bewildered. Having nothing else to do, I asked her where she was from.

"I live in Jerusalem, but I was born in Austria. The Nazis took my family to Auschwitz when I was sixteen and my sister was thirteen. We were in Auschwitz for six months. You see," she announced, as she rolled up her left sleeve and revealed a row of blue tattooed numbers, inscribed by Nazi butchers. "I was a _____ when I was there."

I did not understand the word that she used. In fact, I was not even sure what language it was in. The entire scene in which I found myself was becoming more and more bizarre. Instead of responding to my simple question with an answer like, "I'm from France," this woman was reliving her travails from sixty years ago with the Nazis. For a brief moment, I wondered why this often happened to me. I could be sitting

Tuning In

on a bus or airplane, minding my own business, and people would tell me the most personal and private details of their lives.

"I don't know what that word means," I finally responded. "What is a _____?"

"There were sixty-eight of us in one room when we were in Auschwitz. I used to go into the kitchen every night and steal food. Otherwise, we would have starved to death. The Nazi guard used to catch me and beat me, but from beatings one didn't die. From lack of food, people died. So I was a _____; I used to steal food and give it to everyone so that they would live."

"Did any of your family survive the war?" I asked, now looking with interest, and even awe, at this former "old lady" who was a true heroine. How easily I could have simply dismissed her as an irrelevant elderly person, reminiscing about her past, as so many Americans do when they encounter older people. I was glad that I had started chatting with her.

"We all survived the war. Did you ever hear of a man named Oskar Schindler? He was a drunk, and his wife was a drunk, yet he took me and my sister. There we had food to eat. He took care of us until the end of the War."

By this time, my head was spinning. Nobody understands why this alcoholic, gambling gentile took it upon himself to save hundreds of Jewish souls, all the while hobnobbing with the Nazis. Her amazing story prompted me to wonder why God had put me in the airport, next to this woman, hearing her remarkable story, at that time. The answer came soon enough.

"Do you know how far it is from the plane to the baggage claim in Baltimore's airport?" the woman continued.

"No," I replied, "why do you ask?"

"You see, I was visiting my grandchildren in Netanya (a city near Tel Aviv) a few weeks ago, and my feet got cut while we were walking on the beach. They got terribly infected. In fact, it was so bad, my doctor said that I might die if I didn't get them amputated. So I went to Laniado Hospital. Do you know Laniado Hospital? It's the best hospital in the

What Goes Around, Comes Around

world. The doctor there put me on massive doses of antibiotics. Most people couldn't take so much, but I have a very strong stomach. After three weeks, my feet were almost back to normal. See? It's just a little hard for me to walk long distances."

I looked down at the feet that had carried her into the Auschwitz kitchen every night so that she could steal food for starving inmates. Both were a bit swollen, but not remarkably so. It was hard to imagine that just a few weeks before, they looked as if they needed to be amputated. In a moment, I understood that the Almighty must have regarded her feet as too precious to amputate. He had arranged for her to be healed at the hospital of the Klausenburger Rebbe, the same man who took off his own socks and gave them to a girl so that she would have coverings for her legs.

After hearing this woman's story, I was speechless. I thought about the emotional and physical fortitude that allowed her to endure unspeakable horrors. I thought about how, surrounded by evil, she chose to express her inner divinity. In a place of almost total dehumanization and brutality, she had made herself into an angel. She had chosen to become a model of the nobility of which people are capable despite the hell that raged around her. I felt God's embrace as He showed me how His compassion plays out in His world, even in the darkest, most painful moments. The sterile, empty airport had seemed devoid of His Presence just moments earlier. It was now flooded with a light that far surpassed that which came from the early morning rays of the sun. At the time when I had felt at a loss to connect to my Heavenly Father, He was unmistakably connecting to me.

Part V:
Journeys of the Soul

It's Not Your Time Yet

I became fascinated with the topic of near-death experiences some twenty-five years ago. I often wondered if there were any substantiated reasons to believe that we had souls that went to an afterlife, and I found reports of near-death experiences very reassuring. On the other hand, I had not personally met anyone who had experienced an NDE – or at least, no one who had such an experience had ever discussed it with me.

During a trip to Israel, my husband and I were sitting at a friend's Sabbath table with a dozen or so other people. When I mentioned the topic of near-death experiences, my husband said that he was very skeptical that such phenomena really existed. After all, he had never met anyone who had had an NDE, so he didn't believe in them.

Almost on cue, the woman across the table from him retorted, "I had a near-death experience." Although I had met many people who knew others who had had near-death experiences, this was my first opportunity to speak to someone firsthand about it.

"Please tell us about it," I requested.

"Well," Regina began, "I grew up in California in a totally secular Jewish home. So I wasn't raised with any concept of God or religion. When I was six years old, my brother and I went to the beach with our family. It was a swimming beach, with clean sand and small waves that brought white foam into the shoreline. The water was clean and cold,

Tuning In

and felt so nice on a hot, summer day. Unfortunately, the size of the waves was deceiving. A minute after I stepped into the water, the ocean swept me under with such force that I couldn't get out. My eight-year-old brother was standing next to me one minute, and then I was gone the next. He realized that I must be drowning and frantically screamed for help. In the meantime, he understood that there was no time to waste, and he tried to save me himself. He groped for me under the waves, but it was hard to see me under the foamy swell of waves and murky, sandy water. Time and again he lunged toward a glimpse of my bathing suit, but he never succeeded in making contact with me. Finally, he latched onto my limp arm, but by that time my body was no longer thrashing in the surf. I was dead.

"When I died, I felt my soul leave my body and travel through a tunnel of light. At the other end was what I knew was God. It was so beautiful there, I still remember that feeling today. I felt totally loved and at peace. Meanwhile, I was aware that my brother was trying to save me and bring me back into his world, but I didn't want him to do it. It was so wonderful in the next world that I didn't want to return to this one. I tried to scream at him to leave me alone, to let me be, but it didn't work. I sensed him grabbing my body, and I felt very angry with him for trying to save me. He managed to drag me out of the water, and then some adults who came to help him resuscitated me.

"I was so angry at my brother for bringing me back here that I didn't speak to him for two years. After having my near-death experience, I have never been afraid to die because I know how beautiful it is on the other side."

When we got back to New York, my husband related this story to a medical worker at his hospital. Jane replied, "That's almost exactly what happened to me when I was the same age. I was swimming in a pool and I drowned. My soul went through a tunnel of light and I felt God's Presence and His love when I reached the other side. Meanwhile, my brother tried to rescue me, but I was quite happy where I was. He succeeded, despite my wishes, and I was resuscitated. Here I am today.

"By the way, I'm not afraid to die, either. It really was quite beautiful in the next world."

When my husband told me Jane's story, I began to wonder how many people I knew had also had near-death experiences, but had kept them to themselves. I was soon to find out.

After I returned from my vacation in Israel, I went back to my usual routine of treating psychotherapy patients. While most of the patients in my practice seemed to get better, one patient seemed to encounter one setback after another. Her problems were becoming almost insurmountable, and I wondered if she would ever find her way out of the terrible maze in which she had become trapped.

Jenny had grown up in a dysfunctional family with an authoritarian father and an unstable mother. Jenny had rebelled against them as a teenager and became a hippie. She then met a man in Berkeley, California, who had also rebelled against his rigid parents, and together they traveled by motorcycle across the United States, ending up in Greenwich Village. By the time Jenny was twenty-five, she and Todd decided to settle down and get married. She started working, but he never did. She ended up supporting them both while he spent his days sleeping until noon, then hanging out with his friends. By the end of their first year of marriage, he had racked up $15,000 in credit card debt while she desperately tried to pay off the finance charges and nineteen-percent interest from her secretary's salary.

Not only did she have Todd's financial irresponsibility to contend with, she soon discovered that she was pregnant. She had a very difficult pregnancy and lost her job due to repeated absences at work. To add insult to injury, her mother called periodically to verbally abuse her, and her landlord gave her notice that she would be evicted if she didn't ante up the past two months' rent. She flew into a panic. After all, her baby was due imminently and she had nowhere to go.

A month after she had the baby, Jenny found herself eating compulsively and she retained the forty pounds that she had gained during pregnancy. She had few job skills, was now $25,000 in debt, and had no one to take care of the baby so that she could finish a degree

Tuning In

and get decent employment. A psychiatrist gave her medication for her depression and anxiety, yet she still slept poorly and had passive thoughts of suicide.

"If it weren't for my daughter," she confided in me one bleak day, "I would have killed myself by now." She was only twenty-nine years old.

Soon afterward, Jenny and a close girlfriend took a two-hour drive to visit a mutual friend. On the way home that night, a drunk driver traveling in the opposite direction hit their car head-on. The car spun wildly, crashed through a metal railing on the side of the rural highway, and flew over the embankment. Jenny was thrown from the car and severely injured. The highway was not lit and there were no homes for several miles. Cellular phones didn't exist then, and her girlfriend, who was only bruised, was unable to summon help. Meanwhile, Jenny died.

She felt her soul separate from her body. It hovered above her battered body, now clothed in a tattered, blood-soaked pastel dress. She vividly saw the red stains on her formerly pristine outfit, even though the night was pitch black. She saw her friend as plainly as if it were day, then she felt her soul ascend. It went through a tunnel with a bright light at the end. As she emerged, her uncle stood waiting to greet her with a warm smile. She felt very accepted and loved.

Her uncle had been the most loving relative Jenny had ever had. Unfortunately, he had passed away when she was fourteen, and she had missed him very much since that time. When he greeted her, she was so happy to see him! At that moment, she felt that at long last her misery had finally ended. She would no longer have to deal with a financially irresponsible husband, debts, poor living arrangements, and no job. She would never again feel depressed or anxious. She would not have to send out any more resumes! She wouldn't even have to seek another place to live. Or, so she thought.

"Jenny," her uncle's soul greeted hers, "I'm so happy to see you. But you must know that it's not yet time for you to be here. You have a lot more work to do in the world that you came from. You can't stay here. You'll have to go back."

Journeys of the Soul

That was the last thing that Jenny wanted to hear. She was finally so comfortable, so at peace, and she had to give it all up?!

Before she could object, another scene was taking place. Another driver had traveled the same highway that she had been on, and he had seen the terrible car accident. When he got to the next town, he called an ambulance. The medics arrived and frantically tried to revive Jenny's battered body. They miraculously succeeded moments after her uncle told her that it was not time for her to be in the next world. Jenny felt her soul leave her uncle's presence and return to her body.

The last thing that she wanted was to be alive again. She felt excruciating pain all over her body. The medics had to immobilize her, put her on a stretcher, carry her to the ambulance, and drive her to a hospital a half-hour away. Every bump sent new waves of pain coursing through her. She was soon to find out that she had sustained multiple fractures to a variety of bones in her body, and would have to spend many months in a rehabilitation hospital. She regretted being alive and wished that she could rejoin her uncle.

Jenny's recovery was painfully slow and guarded. To add insult to injury, during her rehabilitation, her previous problems only got compounded. Her husband didn't work so he could take care of their infant, but he had to move in with a friend. She got no job offers to the resume that she had circulated before her accident. To make matters worse – as if that were possible – she was also very depressed. After an absence of six months, Jenny came back to see me.

She hobbled into my office, using a cane. She spent most of our first session after her accident telling about her rehabilitation. Shortly before the session would end, I raised the question of whether or not she'd had a near-death experience. She admitted rather sheepishly that she had, although left to her own devices, she never would have mentioned it to me.

"Why wouldn't you have said anything about it?" I asked, thinking that dying and coming back to life was pretty significant.

Tuning In

"I thought that it was too weird to talk about," she confessed. Based on what I had read, that seemed to be a common sentiment among people who had had NDEs.

"Has your experience changed your life?" I continued. Most people who have had NDEs are affected in important ways. Apart from not being afraid of dying, they generally become more loving, less concerned about trivial things, and often seek knowledge as well.

"I guess the most profound effect it had was making me realize that I can't run away from my problems. I guess that I'm here for a purpose, and I won't leave this world until I do my job."

Jenny stopped seeing me a few weeks later. "I don't need to come here right now," she proclaimed. "I need to get on with my life."

And she did. Over the course of the next several years, her relationship with her husband stabilized, she became a loving and capable mother, and she got back on her feet financially. She also finished her physical rehabilitation and her depression lifted.

One day, Jenny came to see me to discuss a specific problem that she had been having. After we finished what she had set out to do, I asked her how she saw herself and her life.

She laughed. "I never thought that I'd be saying this, but the miracle of dying and recovering was probably the best thing that ever happened to me. My uncle was right. I had a lot of work to do. It's been tough, but it's also been gratifying to see that I could get my act together. For the first time in my life, I really like who I am. My husband was great during my recuperation, and I appreciate him in a different way than I ever did. I am so in love with my daughter. I never thought that I'd find being a mother so gratifying. And, most surprising to me, I even enjoy my work! I never before had a job that I liked. I guess my terrible experience was a small price to pay for all of this."

Sometimes, in the bleakest of moments, a silver lining has been planted. It is just waiting to be discovered.

From Here to Eternity

It was a fall morning on a Saturday in Jerusalem. At 7:30, Leah was about to get dressed. The rest of her household was already buzzing. Her husband Eli and their seven children (twelve and younger) were preparing to go to synagogue services. Leah, a petite woman in her seventh month of pregnancy, was very conscious of her swollen belly, and the tiny baby that was moving inside her. All of a sudden, she felt intense pain instead of the small, jabbing movements that had been her frequent companions for weeks. She knew that she wasn't in labor, but could not imagine what was causing such agony.

Luckily, she lived close to a small hospital. She and her husband rushed to the emergency room while the older children herded the smaller ones behind and followed. In a matter of minutes, the doctors diagnosed her as having a ruptured spleen, which was causing massive bleeding. Most of the blood in her body was quickly pooling in her abdomen instead of flowing through her blood vessels. She needed nine pints of blood just to replace the blood that was lost. At the same time, her unborn baby was in severe distress and had to be delivered immediately by Caesarian section.

To make matters worse, the hospital had no blood of her rare type to give her. Her husband had to race to another hospital some fifteen minutes away in order to procure the blood that might save her life. As the doctors rushed her into surgery, someone took her vital signs. The last words that she heard were from a panicked nurse exclaiming, "She has no pulse."

Tuning In

Leah was whisked into surgery as the doctors attempted to sew up her spleen, stem her bleeding, and deliver her baby. The baby was in terrible distress, having fluid in his lungs from which he developed an infection. Frantic phone calls were made to find a neonatal unit that could treat him. The best-equipped hospital with incubators in the area regretted to inform the caller that all of their incubators were in use and none were available. The second hospital that was contacted had one that was potentially available, but it was reserved for a woman who was in labor. The doctors thought that if her baby would survive long enough, he would need it. As Leah's tiny baby, weighing less than three pounds, fought for his life, the doctors connected him to a tiny ventilator. A doctor hand-pumped air into the newborn's lungs in order to keep him alive.

While Eli sped to bring back the blood that might save Leah's life, Leah was busy traveling as well. As her soul left her lifeless body, it peered down on the surgical suite. She could see the doctors and nurses busily trying to save her and her baby, and she watched the goings-on of the surgery. Soon, her soul traveled along a corridor, which she understood was not in the hospital. (The hospital had only two surgery rooms and no corridor.) At the end of this tunnel was a light. When she arrived at the light, she saw deceased relatives whom she recognized by having seen their pictures. She heard a voice telling her that everything would be okay, and she felt very comfortable.

Back at the hospital, a doctor hurried past the line of seven little children in the waiting room, anxiously hoping that their mother would be saved. The doctor felt choked up as he averted his eyes and thought, "Those poor orphans. Who will take care of them now?"

Just then, Eli ran through the emergency room entrance bearing a box-load of blood. The doctors set up the transfusion into Leah's corpse as quickly as they could. Normally, one can only live for a few minutes without oxygen before brain damage occurs. She had been given plasma but, for a few minutes, that had not been enough to sustain her. The doctors were racing against the clock to see if they could bring her back to life.

Meanwhile, Leah's soul was feeling very serene. She was quite content to stay where she was. The next thing she knew, her soul came back to her body and she was revived. She recovered for the next seven hours. As soon as she opened her eyes, her daughter was sitting next to her. Leah was unsure if her baby could have survived. She asked her daughter, "What happened to my baby?"

When Leah was told the good news, she was unable to believe that her baby was alive. As soon as she could be moved, she saw him for herself.

While Leah's soul had journeyed elsewhere, the hospital staff had been so intent on saving her baby's life that someone had hand-pumped his ventilator for eight hours. Toward the end of that time, the regional hospital called to say that the woman in labor had delivered a healthy baby and her baby did not need the incubator. They put Leah's tiny infant into an ambulance and took him to the hospital where he was placed in the incubator. There, he was finally attached to a mechanical respirator. Still, he was not out of the woods. The doctors told Eli that the baby had been deprived of oxygen for a long time, and he had swelling of the brain. They had no hope that he could recover without significant brain damage. He was tiny and desperately ill, but with lots of prayers and good medical care he recuperated and thrived.

There is no way to describe the relief that baby Yosef's parents felt when he was finally released from the hospital. They had never imagined when Leah was rushed into emergency surgery that a day would come when not only would she be back to excellent health, but that Yosef would be, too.

In recognition of the double miracle that the Almighty made for them, Eli and Leah go every year to the hospital where she and her child nearly died. They commemorate their good fortune by standing outside and reciting a blessing thanking God for making a miracle for them at that place.

When Yosef turned eighteen, he wanted to carry out his army service in Israel as a paratrooper. In order to be accepted, he had to be in excellent physical condition. For the first time in his life, he noticed that it was difficult to run as much as was necessary to pass the requirements. He went to a doctor who assessed his lungs, and he informed Yosef that only forty percent of his lungs were functioning. Apparently, his lungs had been severely damaged due to his birth ordeal but had never impacted on his life until he was taxed with the rigors of intensive running. Today, Yosef is physically and mentally healthy. Despite not being a paratrooper, he has found ways to use his great intelligence to serve his country.

When Leah recalls her doubly miraculous experience, she relates it to the time that it happened. Every Sabbath, Jews read a portion of the Torah, and they try to connect events of the week to that portion. On the Sabbath that Leah died and was revived, and that her son's life was saved, Jews read a Torah portion in the book of Genesis. It tells how God asked Abraham to leave his homeland, his family, and his friends to start a new life in the land that the Almighty would show him. Without questioning the wisdom of abandoning everything that was familiar and comforting to him, Abraham obeyed. This was one of Abraham's ten Divinely engineered tests that challenged and developed him into the great person he became, and which also accrued him great merit.

Like Abraham, Leah also left the place that she grew up, her family and her American friends in order to live in Israel. She credits that sacrifice with giving her the merit to survive a near-death experience and like Abraham, be blessed with a child despite all odds.

Part VI:
Money Matters

Mary's Message

At one time, I treated patients in a psychiatry clinic of a large metropolitan hospital. While I liked many of them, some were so unpleasant that spending forty-five minutes together once a week felt unbearable. Nevertheless, I realized that Divine providence chose which patients came to my office. Ostensibly, my job was to help them have more productive, satisfying lives. Yet the Master of the World wanted my relationship with them to be a two-way street. There were many lessons I could teach them, but just as many that I needed to learn.

One of the first lessons I needed to learn was that earning a living is not simply a matter of working hard, developing a referral network, and currying favor with other professionals. Judaism teaches that the amount of money one will earn is determined at the outset of every year (on the Jewish New Year). In addition, one receives back whatever one spends to honor the Sabbath and Jewish holidays.

This sounded nice in theory, but when I started my professional career, I wasn't so sure that it worked in practice. While I'm not guaranteeing that those who follow my model will have the same outcome, the results that I experienced certainly taught me a strong lesson.

Shortly after I started working at my new hospital job, my boss taught me everything that he thought I should know about starting a private practice.

"You must order announcement cards and send them to everyone on this list," he advised. Since he was twenty years my senior, and had

Tuning In

been running a lucrative private practice for years, I followed his recommendations. I bought beautifully printed announcement cards, enclosed a few business cards in each envelope, and dutifully mailed them off to the list of doctors that he provided. During the next six years, I never received a single referral as a result of that mailing. I later discovered that most of the doctors' secretaries had filed those envelopes as promptly as they could in their garbage cans.

A few years after I established an ongoing practice of ten to fifteen patients a week, I began to notice a pattern. If a patient came once or twice a week, then stopped coming, it meant a potential income loss of thousands of dollars in the course of a year. I realized that many therapists had a vested interest in never terminating with their patients, or at least in delaying the process for as long as possible. If someone believes that their income depends on retaining as many patients as they can for as long as they can, that is a strong motivator to make sure that patients don't leave. On the other hand, if we believe that God provides our earnings, but we must work hard and ethically to create channels for Him to give it to us, we may treat patients very differently. My philosophy of doing therapy was to give patients the tools they needed to live more effectively, and then gently turn them out of my office and into the real world. Helping patients to get better, though, was very risky financially. Every time the patient won, my bank account lost – theoretically. I had to trust the Almighty to make the balance sheets work.

And they did, much to my amazement. I rarely strongly urged patients to stay in therapy when they cited good reasons for terminating. Many therapists intimidate or pressure their patients into continuing, using a variety of psychological tools to convince them that they have much more emotional work to do. I tended to wish my patients well, and tell them the door was always open should they feel the need for future help.

It was unsettling to realize that when one patient stopped therapy, my income could plummet hundreds of dollars that month. Yet there were weeks when two, or even three of my patients, for totally

Money Matters

unanticipated reasons, might terminate at the same time. There were times when thirty percent of my patients disappeared overnight. At first, that frightened me. Then I began to understand that the Comptroller of the world was using my profession to teach me about Divine providence.

One week started as follows: Sally, a soft-spoken woman in her late twenties, had been seeing me for six months to help her bolster her self-esteem and overcome her depression. She was well on her way to accomplishing both. That Monday, she came to my office and announced that she was moving to Appalachia to teach underprivileged children. She would be starting her new position in four weeks, and was stopping work that week. She could manage only two more sessions before we terminated, and she wanted to see me during her lunch break instead of during her usual after-work slot. I agreed to reschedule her.

That afternoon, I got a telephone call from a friend of my patient Louise. Betty had been meaning to call me for months, but she kept hoping that her problems would resolve themselves. Lately, things had just reached a breaking point and she couldn't go on that way much longer. Did I have any openings in my practice to see her?

Of course I did. I fit her into Sally's old slot.

The next day, Barry, a patient who had been seeing me weekly for several months, came for his appointment. He divulged that he had been fired from his job, and he didn't have enough savings to continue therapy. Despite my suggestion that we work out a payment plan so that he could get emotional support and guidance while he looked for work, he was adamant. He had to bite the financial bullet so that he didn't pile up debts. He would call me when he was working again.

My last patient that day, Ellen, was given an ultimatum by her boyfriend of two years. Either they get engaged within a month, or he was going to stop seeing her and start dating others. She was in a panic and couldn't make up her mind about what she should do. Could I see her twice a week for the next month so that she could get help making her decision?

Tuning In

Thursday morning, my first patient was Ed. He had been seeing me once a week for a year, and we had an excellent relationship. His insurance company was now insisting that I file a detailed treatment plan for his continued therapy or they would no longer pay for his sessions. Ed was a bit of a public figure, and was terrified that any information that I divulged to the insurance company might not stay confidential. The last thing that he wanted was for people to know personal details of his life. Ed was a bit paranoid anyway, so he dismissed my reassurances that his fears would not be realized. He decided that rather than pay out of pocket for therapy, he would muddle through life as best he could without any more help.

As soon as Ed left, my telephone rang. A former patient of mine, whom I hadn't seen in a year, was having a family crisis. Could she and her sister see me together for a few sessions?

And so it went, year after year. The same number of patients who dropped out of therapy were usually replaced by exactly the same number of new patients by the end of the week. I realized that how much I earned only depended on my working honestly and being available to make money when opportunities arose. Extra efforts that I made to increase my referrals never bore fruit.

One day, a colleague told me that I should get to know the doctors when they ate lunch in the doctor's dining room at the hospital. I ate lunch there almost every day for two months and introduced myself to a variety of physicians who might have reason to refer their patients for help. Many were interested in the interface between the type of psychological services that I provided and medicine. Nevertheless, I never got a single referral from the people I met there. On the other hand, I received a number of referrals from hospital doctors who came to me through channels that had nothing to do with my efforts.

Judaism teaches that one must make appropriate efforts to try to earn a living and do what is normally done to procure an honest income. On the other hand, we should never think that we do more than make the effort. The outcome is always a manifestation of Divine providence giving us exactly what we need.

Money Matters

After working for the Veteran's Administration and two city hospitals for eight years, I began to feel as if my talents could be put to better use if I worked full-time in private practice. I was tired of hospital politics and administration and wanted to devote myself to treating private patients. On the other hand, my hospital job was cushy, the pay was very good, and my position funneled many private patients my way. As months turned into years and I stayed at my salaried job, I became increasingly dissatisfied. I felt that I was wasting a lot of time doing tasks that I considered unimportant. And yet, I was terrified to leave because I had never developed referral networks with any professionals outside of the hospital.

I learned during my many years as a therapist that the Master of the World often communicated with me via my patients, yet it often took me a long time to hear and internalize those messages. One of the most unlikely messengers He ever sent me was Mary. I could not have imagined anyone with whom I had less in common. Mary was twenty-five years my senior, from a devout, Irish Catholic family. She had been an alcoholic for twenty years, but had stayed sober thanks to her daily attendance at Alcoholics Anonymous meetings for the past fifteen years. She had been hospitalized twelve times in as many years, and had only been out of hospital for two years. She had received every diagnosis in the book, and then some. She had been given electroshock treatment, drugs for schizophrenia, lithium for manic-depression, anti-anxiety medications, and drugs whose sole purpose seemed to be to make money for the hospital pharmacy. It was not clear what problems had gotten her into these hospitals in the first place, but she vowed that she was never going back. By the time she came to me, she refused to take any medications, complained of chronic pain in most parts of her body, and ranted nonstop in rapid-fire speech about everyone and everything. Mary was one of the angriest non-violent people whom I have ever met.

Mary usually spent about forty-three of our forty-five minutes together raging about everyone's incompetence and about the injustices – real and imagined – that she suffered. She didn't want

Tuning In

to hear any responses from me. She viewed our time together as her opportunity to have a paid professional listen to her without comment. I quickly learned that to interrupt her with anything more than a question or a nod would unravel her fragile train of thought and release a torrent of condemnation.

I couldn't reduce Mary to a simple diagnosis, although it was clear that she was schizophrenic with paranoid traits. Yet she sometimes shocked me by coming up with profound statements that I later pondered. I initially hated working with her because she was so ungrateful, so angry, and so unwilling to use me for any purpose other than being a silent listener. Yet another part of me knew that there was something each of us should be gaining from our sessions. I knew that I was the only person she had ever had in her life who would listen uncritically to her and let her vent her rage. In the two years that I saw her, she never took any medications, never hallucinated, never needed to be hospitalized, and never had an alcoholic drink. I knew that something about my "treatment" must have worked. Emotionally, though, I wanted her to get past where she was, and that certainly wasn't what she wanted. I soon came to see that God had a different agenda than I had for my sessions with Mary.

After treating her for about six months, Mary insisted on coming twice a week for sessions. As I had an open slot for a patient in the clinic, I agreed. I then listened to her tirades twice a week and felt totally drained each time she left.

In November that year, Mary announced that she would not be able to schedule future sessions with me for an unknown period of time.

"You see," she said unequivocally, "it's getting cold outside and I have no winter coat. I have to save my disability money until I can buy myself one. Once I do, I'll come back. Until then, I can't afford the fifteen dollars that it costs me to come here. I'm not sure when I'll be back, but I'll call you when I have the money to return."

Mary had been so difficult to work with, and so miserly with her appreciation for anyone who helped her, that I was secretly relieved to have a respite from her anger. I soon discovered that my respite was to be short-lived. By the end of our session, Mary reconsidered.

"You know, Dr. Aiken, God always wants me to take care of myself. One way that I take care of myself is by coming here and seeing you. I don't have a penny in the bank right now, but I know that I need to keep my appointments here. Give me my usual appointment for next week and I'll be here. You see, one thing that I've learned from my life is that God always provides. I know that I can always count on Him. I have no idea where I'll get the money from to buy a coat and also see you, but I'm sure that He'll take care of it."

A little disappointed, I penned Mary's name in my schedule book for the following week. As far as I knew, Mary had no sources of income other than her Social Security disability. She had already spent it for the month of November. She had no friends from whom she could get a loan. Where in the world, I wondered, would she get enough money to pay for a coat as well as for her therapy appointments?

The next week, like clockwork, Mary appeared for her session wearing a slightly worn fur coat.

"I'll bet you're wondering where I got this from, aren't you, Doc?" she prodded. I had learned not to respond to her questions with anything more than a look of interest and a nod.

"Well, after I left here last week, I went across the street to the house of worship. I got down on my knees and asked God to please help me. As soon as I got up, the priest came over and asked, 'Mary, do you need a winter coat? A very wealthy lady from the neighborhood came here last night. She told me that she had a fur coat that she wasn't using anymore. She asked me if I knew anyone who needed a winter coat. I told her that I didn't, but that I was sure it wouldn't take long to find someone who did. So, Mary, can you use this coat?' And that, Dr. Aiken, is how I got this.

"See," she concluded triumphantly, "I told you that God always provides."

Here was a woman who had very little in life. When I first read her psychiatric reports, I pitied her. Her family had rejected her; she

Tuning In

had not worked in twenty years. She lived from month to month on disability payments. She had few friends. That day, I realized that she considered herself very blessed. Due to the very vicissitudes and challenges for which I had pitied her, she had grown into a woman of enormous faith.

I felt humbled sitting across from her.

I was afraid to leave my lucrative position at the hospital because I could not trust that God would provide for me. For Mary, life was a series of episodes of Divine providence.

I heard the lesson that was meant for me, but I was still skeptical.

Staying at the hospital was becoming increasingly untenable for me, and I felt it was seriously compromising my emotional and spiritual well- being. And yet, what alternative did I have? My job provided me with health insurance and was the basis for my long-standing, part-time private practice. It also gave me two months of paid vacation a year. How could I leave?

When the Master of the World saw that, a month later, I still had not internalized Mary's lesson, He sent me her message again. It was now two weeks before Xmas, and Mary barreled into my office.

"It's getting close to the holidays, and I won't be able to come for my regular appointments for a few weeks. You see, God wants me to take care of myself, and the way that I do that this time of year is to buy myself Xmas presents. I don't have enough money to buy myself gifts and also pay my fifteen dollars here at the clinic. So I'll call you in a few weeks when I have enough money to come back."

I smiled, thinking that I was going to have a break from Mary's tirades for a few weeks. My respite again turned out to be very short-lived. By the end of the session she announced, "God always wants me to take care of myself. One way that I take care of myself is by coming here to see you. Give me my usual appointment and I'll see you Thursday. One thing that I've learned in my life is that God always provides. I don't know how it's going to happen, but I'm not worried. God is powerful enough that He can do anything."

Money Matters

I heard her pronouncement, but I was a bit skeptical. In theory, I believed that God can always provide, but why should He just because Mary said He would? I was curious as to whether Mary would show up in my office later that week.

Like clockwork, Mary came for her 3:00 appointment the following Thursday. After arranging her bags around her chair like flowerpots in a garden, she began.

"Do you remember that I told you my mother and I have not spoken for the past two years? We've had a terrible relationship for many, many years. Well, when I went home from here a few days ago, there was a letter from her in my mailbox. She had enclosed a check for a hundred dollars as an Xmas present. So here I am.

"See, one thing that I've learned from my life is that God always provides. He doesn't always give us what we want, but He always gives us what we need."

This time, I finally learned Mary's lesson. Not long afterward, I left the hospital and worked only in private practice. My referrals from the hospital didn't continue, but within three days, friends of patients whom I hadn't seen in years started calling me. I was soon working ten hours a week less than I had while I was at the hospital, yet I was making almost double the income.

Mary was right. God always gives us what we need. But first, in order to receive His gifts, we sometimes need to have enough trust in Him to take risks and make difficult changes. After I put in my requisite effort, God was right there, holding His hand open for me to take what He so much wanted to give.

The Heavenly Accountant

Some religious Jews make great sacrifices so that the husbands can study Torah in yeshiva (men's college for full-time Torah study) while the wives (or parents) support their learning. Dina and Tuvia, a couple in their late twenties, were such a couple. He studied Torah full-time while she worked part-time as a physical therapist and raised their three young children. Their existence was hand-to-mouth because their expenses roughly equaled their income and they barely made ends meet at the end of the month. Over time, their financial situation deteriorated. One month, their son got sick, and Dina had to take the baby to the doctor more times than they had budgeted. She owed money to the pediatrician. Then she got a bill from the preschool for her daughter's monthly tuition. It had a special assessment tacked on to the usual amount because the school needed to buy supplies. Then she got a bill from her obstetrician. Her insurance had not paid all of the postpartum expenses, and the doctor's office expected Dina to pay the difference. She wrote checks to everyone to whom she owed money, but did not keep track of the total amount that needed to be deducted from her checking account. She felt absolutely overwhelmed by the time she got her bank statement that month and found that she was overdrawn by $642.37. Where in the world would she get that kind of money? She could ask her parents to loan her a hundred dollars, or even borrow fifty here and fifty there from a couple of friends. But how in the world would she ante up $642.37?

Dina was so preoccupied worrying about how to pay her bills that she was not focused on her surroundings. It was time for her to carpool that afternoon. She grabbed her baby, rushed outside to her station wagon, and strapped the baby into his car seat. As she backed out of her driveway, she didn't notice a car going in reverse from the cul-de-sac two houses away. The car smashed into her station wagon and severely dented the rear end of her car.

"Oh, no, not this on top of everything else!" she cried reflexively. She got out and surveyed her damaged car as the other driver got out of his car. His car was barely touched; hers had a pretty nasty-looking dent. She burst into tears and prayed, "Dear God, please help me. I can't deal with my financial problems and this on top of it. Please help me find a way out of this mess." She got the driver's insurance information and planned to file a claim that evening. Meanwhile, the damage to her car looked nasty, but was only cosmetic. She was able to drive the car to the preschool and pick up the children in her carpool.

That evening, she told her husband that he would have to start teaching in order for them to make ends meet. He agreed to look for a job first thing the next morning. In the meantime, she was worried sick about what to do about the bank overdraft. "Look," her husband said, "we're doing the best we can now to make the right efforts to earn an appropriate living. All we can do is to ask God to help us out of this dilemma."

Dina calmed down and prayed that the Almighty would somehow fix their financial problems and get them back on a firmer footing. She couldn't imagine, though, how that could possibly happen.

Her answer came at the end of the week. The insurance adjustor surveyed her car the day after the accident. Dina got a check in the mail from the insurance company a few days later. As she nervously opened the envelope, she couldn't wait to see how much the company had deemed the damage to her car was worth. When she laid eyes on

Money Matters

the amount payable, she couldn't believe what she saw. The amount was precisely $642.37!

Money Matters

All You Have To Do Is Ask

About twenty years ago, a teacher in Jerusalem named Shira Friedman went to visit a neighbor. As Shira chatted with Raizy, Shira was surprised that her neighbor's six-year-old son was home from school. Shira watched the young boy play listlessly with a broken toy.

"Is your son sick?" Shira asked, concerned.

"No," Raizy answered softly as she averted her eyes, "we don't have enough money to buy him a pair of shoes."

Shira was horrified. In the land of Israel, a Jewish child was unable to get an education because his parents were too poor to buy him a pair of shoes. When she went home, Shira couldn't stop thinking about this poor boy and his parents' destitution.

Some people would have simply buried the incident so as not to disturb their inner peace, but not Shira. She started talking to some friends about this terrible situation and their response shook her even more.

"He's not the only child here who has no shoes to wear," one after another told her. As she began to check out their reports, she discovered that abject poverty was epidemic in Jerusalem. A number of mothers were so malnourished that they couldn't nurse their babies. Formula was so expensive that they diluted it with three times as much water as was appropriate, resulting in babies who needed to be hospitalized. Untold numbers of children had hand-me-down shoes.

Tuning In

By the end of the day, their small feet had blisters because the shoes were simply a size or two too small. Families had no food at all in their pantries, and their refrigerators were empty. Children went to bed hungry at night. Some parents split one yogurt between three children and called it dinner. Other families didn't even have chairs in their cramped apartments, and tables doubled as beds at night. One tragedy after another unfolded in front of Shira's eyes as she investigated the dire conditions with which hundreds of families lived day after day.

Instead of simply shrugging her shoulders at the prevalence of this unspeakable poverty, Shira was determined to do something to ameliorate it. Over the next few years, she started a charitable organization to make a dent in the horrific problems. She amassed hundreds of young and old, religious and secular women and men volunteers to help. At the start of every month, volunteers put together baskets of food staples and delivered them to about a thousand families. These emergency packages gave families enough food staples to last them through the month. For the hundreds of families that did not have enough food to even tide them through the week, volunteer women doubled their usual food preparation for the Sabbath. They donated half of these cooked meals to indigent families who then had food on their tables for the Sabbath. Volunteers delivered these food packages every Thursday and helped these families to survive.

Today, this charity is known throughout many cities in Israel as an organization that provides food and other necessities to the poorest of the poor. They distribute about six million dollars worth of fruits and vegetables donated by farmers in various cities to people who could not otherwise afford to buy even carrots, cucumbers or apples. American donors ship three containers a year of shoes and clothing for distribution to thousands of Jerusalem families who can't afford to buy these items.

In addition, this organization makes weddings for poor immigrants and for others with no financial resources. They likewise provide formula for babies whose mothers are too sick, or who are unable, to nurse.

Money Matters

The charity's budget has grown as its number of beneficiaries has swelled. Today, one in every four Israeli children, and one in every five adults lives below the poverty line. That number is expected to rise with the continuing economic problems in Israel. The ongoing terror attacks which have destroyed the tourism business, coupled with the tech wreck, have left hundreds of thousands of workers in this tiny country unemployed, have forced thousands of restaurants, businesses and hotels to close, and have pushed many families beyond their ability to cope.

Shira's American counterpart, Tova, decided years ago to raise much of the money that is needed to feed thousands of such indigent children and adults. Tova realized that by holding a Chinese auction every spring, she could raise enough money to help tide over the charity's beneficiaries through the summer months when donors typically give very little. Holding such an event is a massive undertaking that requires almost a year of many people working together. Soon after one auction is held, it is time to start planning for the next year's affair.

Making sure that every detail is properly taken care of is very stressful. There are an enormous number of details to tend to, including the procuring of nearly one thousand instant prizes. These instant prizes are like raffle prizes. The guests buy as many instant prize tickets as they like, each of which costs a small amount of money. When the buyers scratch off a silver coating, hundreds find that their tickets reveal that the bearer is entitled to a prize worth much more than they paid for the ticket. Since a wide variety of people attend the auction, procuring a proper assortment of prizes that will please everyone is always a difficult and delicate task.

Some people have attended enough auctions that they have won the same instant prizes more than once, necessitating having different instant prizes every year. One year, finding the right quantity of suitable prizes proved very difficult. Tova mentioned to me that she was in dire need of over three hundred prizes.

Tuning In

The year before, I had experienced a series of "coincidences." I had spent a few days with my rabbi's family during a holiday when he and his wife had hosted scores of people. I noticed a man who looked familiar at one of the meals and asked him what kind of work he did.

"I distribute children's toys and clothes," he answered.

"Does your company ever donate goods to charities?" I was brazen enough to ask. I felt very uncomfortable asking people to make donations to charity.

"We do sometimes. Speak to my secretary during the week. Her name is Cheryl. See if she can help you." I felt uncomfortable prolonging the conversation beyond that point. I wasn't sure if his comment was a way of brushing me off, or if Cheryl might actually help us find what we needed.

I felt both anticipation and apprehension when I called Cheryl the following Monday morning. I could feel her excitement over the telephone as I described why I was calling, and the type of work that Shira's charity did. She was very eager to help in any way that she could.

"Let me do an inventory at the warehouse when I get a chance and I'll see if we have any overstocks or outdated items. The company will be happy to donate any such items as long as you are willing to pick them up."

She was such a sweetie, I felt happy just talking to her! I tried to rein in my excitement, though, because who knew what her inventory would show?

Cheryl got back to me later that week with news that made my heart soar. She had gotten orders to clear out the warehouse during the next two weeks and restock it with new merchandise. I could take whatever I wanted for the organization.

When I arrived, I felt like I had been invited to a treasure hunt. There were hundreds of baby outfits in pastel pinks, greens, blues and yellows. Each was made of soft, combed cotton. There were baby blankets, covered with teddy bear emblems, balloons, and clouds. Still other boxes were filled with gift sets containing baby bottles, washcloths, bibs, teething rings and toys. There were stacks of plush teddy bears. In the corner were piles of children's clothes, packed into cartons. I practically danced with joy at the thought that hundreds of infants and children would have clean, beautiful clothes to wear. Children who would otherwise grow up without ever holding a teddy bear or doll of their own would now have one.

A worker helped me move the booty out of the warehouse and into my car. Even after tying boxes onto the roof racks and packing every nook and cranny with merchandise, I had not packed half the items. I would need to borrow a neighbor's van and make a second trip. What a wonderful problem to have! I fairly sailed home with what I had, elated to have to go back again.

When I later unpacked and sorted the clothes, I realized, to my horror, that every item of clothing had been slashed with a razor blade. Each had also been stamped "Not for sale" with purple ink! (This had to be done in order to avoid paying import taxes on samples that would not be sold.) My dreams of clothing hundreds of children were shattered in a moment. I wanted to cry, but I felt that I didn't have the luxury of doing that. I needed to see if there were any salvageable items to send to Israel and for instant prizes for the auction.

As I carefully sorted through the gift sets and toys, and set some aside for the auction, an idea popped into my head. I had sewn my own clothes as a teenager, and I had recently bought a brand-new sewing machine in order to make curtains and maternity dresses. Perhaps this new machine could invisibly stitch the gaps in the garments that I had just procured? It was certainly worth a gamble. I went furiously to work setting up the sewing machine and trying my hand at slash repair.

Hours later, at 2:00 in the morning, I blearily surveyed my work. I was exhausted, but felt the adrenalin surging through my body as my brain told me that I had been victorious against massive odds. I had salvaged all but three of the outfits and had carefully washed away the ink stamps. I packed the clothes into boxes to be shipped overseas. The next morning, I brought the remaining prize boxes to Tova in Brooklyn.

Tuning In

When she saw the prizes, her eyes gleamed with delight. They were just enough to complete the number of instant prizes that she would need at the auction, now a mere two weeks away.

For the next two years, Cheryl called me periodically to tell me that I could clear out some outdated merchandise. Tova and I were so grateful to her, and to her boss, for bettering the lives of so many children.

The following year, I tried to help Tova by contacting national organizations to see if they would contribute goods, services, or sponsorships for the auction. Nothing I did panned out. I received one rejection letter after another from banks, cosmetics companies, and children's clothing manufacturers and distributors. Tova was also having an extremely difficult time getting enough instant prizes that year. I could feel the strain she was under every time that I spoke to her. By now, there were thousands of indigent people depending on the success of the auction. If the auction did not raise enough money, they would not have food on their table or shoes on their feet. I wanted so much to help Tova, but I felt that my hands were tied.

One night, I was leaving my Manhattan office and riding the subway to Penn Station as I always did after work. Even though it was 8:00 P.M., the train was very crowded, and I had to stand alongside many other straphangers. As we approached the next station, the conductor slammed on the brakes, and a sudden jolt knocked me into a woman. As I apologized and pulled my face out of the folder she was holding, I noticed the company logo on the cover of her clipboard. I recognized the name of the company as a well-known toy manufacturer. After I regained my footing, I asked her if her company ever donated their children's toys to charities.

"Yes, I'm sure we do." She smiled benevolently, not the least bit perturbed by either my fall or my question. "Call this number and ask for the charitable donations department," she said, pointing to the number under her company's logo. With that, she gave me her company card.

Money Matters

In the seven minutes that it took to ride from my office to the train station, providence had arranged for me to bump into a ministering angel. The next day, I called her company. Sure enough, the woman who ran the charitable donations department would make it possible for us to buy three-hundred prizes, each valued at twenty or more dollars, for a mere two dollars apiece.

A few months after that year's auction, Tova and I confronted a new set of problems. I noticed that Cheryl had not called me for a long time, and the company from which I had purchased the prizes the year before had raised their prices beyond what we could afford. Six months before the next auction, I called Cheryl, only to find out that she was no longer with her company. I tried to explain to her replacement who I was, and what Cheryl used to do for the charity. Melanie was totally uninterested in hearing about it.

"I don't know anything about this. If you have any problems, you'll have to talk to Mr. Stein." That was followed by a tense silence, then a curt "Goodbye."

I had not spoken to Ronnie Stein, her boss, for years. It was very difficult for me to bother him as I knew that he ran a multimillion-dollar business and was always on the phone, traveling, or running to take care of some problem. I waited a few minutes, took a deep breath, then called Melanie back.

"Hi, can I speak to Mr. Stein, please?" I asked politely.

"Who's calling?" a no-nonsense voice responded.

"It's the lady who called you a few minutes ago about the donations for the charity," I replied as nonchalantly as I could manage.

"I'm sorry, Mr. Stein is not here," she retorted.

Recalling his schedule from Cheryl's descriptions, I knew what to ask. "Is he out of the country?" I inquired.

"Yes," came the monosyllabic reply.

"When will he be back?" I persisted.

"In three weeks," she answered, testily.

Tuning In

I knew that there was no point in leaving a message. I would simply call back in three-and-a-half weeks and hope for the best. I marked it on my calendar.

On the appointed day, I dutifully called Ronnie's number and reached his secretary. "May I speak to Mr. Stein, please?"

"I'm sorry," she responded in a business-like tone. "He's in meetings all day today. Would you care to leave a message?"

"Yes, I would. Please ask Mr. Stein to call me." I then left my name and my phone number.

Another three weeks passed, and I never heard from Ronnie. It was now getting uncomfortably close to the auction, and Tova still needed many more instant prizes. Ronnie's merchandise would have been just what the doctor ordered, but he was totally inaccessible. Week after week passed, with me calling and being told that Ronnie was not available. I still left messages every other time for him to call me back, but I never heard from him. Another two months had passed, and the auction was just around the corner. Tova still needed at least fifty to a hundred more prizes. I could hear the desperation in her voice and felt totally helpless to make her life easier.

Ironically, it had not occurred to me to pray for Divine assistance to solve this dilemma. Until that point, I had felt that if I only tried hard enough, I would be able to get what Tova and the charitable recipients needed. I understood by the number of dead ends that I had reached that there was nothing more that I could do. So, I did what every good person does in a foxhole. I prayed. I asked the Master of the World to please send us, through some means, the prizes that we needed to help His children.

Just as I finished praying, the telephone rang. I assumed that it was the start of the daily round of morning solicitors trying to sell me newspapers, long-distance service and cable TV. I wearily picked up the receiver and blurted out, "Hello."

"Hi, is this Lisa?" the voice inquired.

"Yes," I replied, incredulous. "Ronnie?!"

Money Matters

"Yes," he answered. "I understand that you've been trying to reach me. I'm sorry, but I've been away on business for most of the last four months. I just got your message from three weeks ago this morning. It was buried under some papers on my desk and I just noticed it now. Can I help you in some way?"

"You don't know how happy I am to hear from you. I hope that you can help me. Do you remember that Cheryl used to help me with donations to a charity? They're having their annual auction in a few weeks and they desperately need some more donations. Do you have any gift sets in your warehouse that you could donate?"

I could hear him smile over the telephone. "I'll see what I can do. I can't get there now, but give me a call later this week. If I'm not available, I'll leave a message with Melanie."

On Thursday, Melanie called me. "We have some items here for you to pick up. You'd better have a big van. It looks like there is a lot of stuff for you at the warehouse."

I called Tova with the good news. I could hear her breathe a sigh of relief. She then told me the following, "You know, Shira always tells me, 'Tova, you have everything you need in the palm of your hand. All you have to do is ask for it.'"

We both learned that morning how true that was. When Tova went to pick up the merchandise, there was exactly the number of instant prizes that she still needed for the auction. All we had needed to do was ask.

Part VII:
Brushes with Mortality

The Verdict

Seth was a busy litigator, whose favorite hobby was playing tennis. Every Sunday, his tanned, lean, lanky figure, wearing a contrasting white shirt and shorts, played opposite his next-door neighbor at their country club in Miami. He cut a striking figure with his light blue eyes, high cheekbones, thin lips, and mousy brown hair that was graying at the temples. While some people play tennis to relax, Seth took his intensity with him. He could be soft-spoken about topics that were not important to him, yet he was a formidable opponent in court and on the courts. He never did anything that mattered to him in a devil-may-care way. Whether he won or lost, in or out of court, on or off the courts, mattered very much to him. He took his battles seriously and he hated to lose.

By the time Seth was fifty years old, his tennis game was deteriorating because his right knee was degenerating. The cartilage on the inside of his kneecap had worn away, he had torn several ligaments that had never healed, and his orthopedist had recommended surgery. Despite his chronic pain, Seth kept delaying surgery because he didn't want to miss time at work. He would rather take anti-inflammatory medication as long as possible to avoid the knife, but the relief he got from taking pills was short-lived. He finally decided to check into a hospital and get the surgery over and done with.

The doctor had told him that knee surgery was often an outpatient procedure, but he preferred that Seth stay in the hospital for a few days so that he would be sure to recuperate. Seth checked into the medical facility on Labor Day. At 7:00 the next morning he was rolled

Tuning In

into the surgery suite. The surgery took the usual amount of time and accomplished what it was intended to do. After Seth's knee was revamped, he was moved into the recovery room where the nurses were supposed to monitor him every fifteen minutes.

His wife came to greet him and wasn't surprised that he was drowsy. That was expected after general anesthesia. She sat nearby and waited as he became more alert during the next hour. The nurses thought that he had recovered sufficiently to have him moved to his room, and they called orderlies to relocate him within the hour. In the meantime, he started becoming drowsy again. Just before he was moved, his wife became very concerned and she spoke to the head nurse.

"My husband is Mr. Landau. He was talking to me half an hour ago, and now he seems very sleepy. Is that normal?"

"Yes," the head nurse responded in a condescending voice. "Surgery takes a lot out of people. He probably needs his rest. You just let us take care of him and everything will be fine."

Seth got moved into his semi-private room, all the while not stirring. When the orderlies asked him to roll off the stretcher onto his bed, he didn't respond.

His wife was very concerned. "It's not like my husband not to take charge of things. If he's not cooperating, there must be something wrong." The orderlies ignored her and rolled Seth onto his bed, straightened the sheets around him, and left the room. Seth didn't budge.

His wife, Lynn, became alarmed. She didn't know much about medicine, but something seemed very wrong to her. She pressed the buzzer next to his bed to summon a nurse. Five minutes later a nurse answered, "What's the problem, honey?"

Lynn replied with a tremor in her high-pitched voice, "My husband came out of surgery several hours ago, and he's in such a deep sleep that I can't wake him up."

The nurse, already overwhelmed with many other patients and their relatives, responded, "He just needs time to sleep off his anesthesia. Let him get his rest. We'll be in later to check on him."

Brushes with Mortality

Lynn watched with horror as her husband stayed totally unresponsive. An hour later, his heart monitor alarm rang loudly and his electrocardiogram showed that he was having a heart attack. In the time that it took the team of doctors and nurses to arrive at his bedside, Seth had a cardiac arrest. Although they resuscitated him, he remained in a coma.

What apparently happened during those hours was that the morphine that Seth had been given during his surgery had been absorbed into his spinal fluid and had gone to his brain. When it reached the breathing center of his brain, he went into a coma and stayed there.

His wife kept a vigil at his bedside, but his condition remained poor and unchanged. As days passed, the doctors discussed disconnecting him from life support. At best, if he ever came out of his coma, they insisted that he would be a vegetable. At worst, the most likely scenario, he would never come out of his coma. After ten days, they advised his wife to authorize them to take him off the ventilator. She was adamantly opposed and insisted that doing so was tantamount to murder. She was a religious woman and there was no moral justification for taking him off life-support under the circumstances. The doctors countered that he had no quality of life, he would never have any quality of life, and taking him (and her) out of their misery was the best possible option.

Lynn couldn't reconcile herself to that. How did the doctors know that Seth would never come out of his coma? Some people were in comas longer than ten days and still came back to life. In any event, she wasn't willing to let the doctors play God.

A few more days went by, and the doctors became more and more insistent that Lynn authorize them to disconnect the life support. She kept refusing. The Day of Atonement, the holiest day of the Jewish year, was approaching. She didn't want to make such a grave decision until after the holiday. There would be time then to consult a rabbi and get his input.

Lynn came to the hospital the morning preceding the Day of Atonement, and the doctors came by to examine her husband. They

Tuning In

shook their heads as they reviewed Seth's poorly functioning bodily systems.

"Mrs. Landau, we know that this is very emotional for you, but you have to understand. Your husband has now been in a coma for nearly two weeks. The chances that he will come out of his coma are slim to nil. If he does come out of it, he will not be the man that you once knew. We are pretty sure that he has had a stroke. We know that he has had a heart attack and his heart is no longer as strong as it was. He will never regain his memory. He will not be able to think like an adult. He will have problems with coordination and may not have good muscle control any more. In short, he will be an invalid that someone will have to take care of for the next twenty or thirty years. Do you think that is what your husband wants for himself? Think about it, Mrs. Landau, and let us know when you are ready for us to disconnect him from the ventilator."

Lynn was on the verge of tears, but refused to give her consent. The doctors left the room in disgust. Seth was taking up a hospital bed and was consuming lots of medical resources. Meanwhile, there was nothing more the doctors could do for him. He needed to be transferred to a long-term care facility, not be taking up a bed in an acute medical hospital.

As noon approached, Lynn needed to leave in order to go home and prepare for the Day of Atonement. She kissed her husband, wished him a good holiday, and left.

Later, she and a few family members ate an early dinner at home. At 5:30, they left for services and began the twenty-five hour fast. As the sun set, Lynn stood in her usual place in the women's section of her synagogue. Her thoughts were elsewhere as the cantor began intoning the solemn, haunting prayers that usher in the Day of Atonement. She glanced at her husband's seat in the men's section, and it was conspicuously empty. Every year for the last fourteen years Seth had occupied that seat during the High Holidays. He normally stood there, wrapped in his prayer shawl, as the congregation implored the Almighty's forgiveness. The men wore white caftans on the Day of

Brushes with Mortality

Atonement to remind themselves that they were as pure as angels on this special day. The white also symbolized the white shrouds in which Jews are buried. The Day of Atonement reminds us of the transience and fragility of life. The fact that we could die at any moment motivates us to repent while we still have the opportunity to do so.

As Lynn was lost in thought, a murmur traveled like a wave through the packed synagogue and brought her out of her reverie. Lynn noticed people turning to face the back entrance to the house of prayer. As she turned around, she nearly fainted at what she saw. As her knees buckled, she managed to grab onto the seat in front of her to keep herself from collapsing. Seth had walked in the door and was wending his way to his seat!

He had woken up from his coma two hours before services. He had gotten dressed, checked out of the hospital, and took a taxi to the synagogue. On such short notice, he hadn't had time to dress in special holiday clothes. Yet, he was unmistakably there, joining the rest of the congregation as they prayed.

That Yom Kippur, surely none of the men's white garments were as potent a reminder of the day of death as Seth was. He was a living example of the ideas put forth in the prayers of the Day of Atonement. They assert that the Holy One, Blessed be He, gives life, or takes it away, at any moment, according to His will.

Fireworks, Friends, and the Fourth of July

It was the second week of June. Mitchell sat sweltering in his Manhattan studio apartment on a Sunday morning when his phone rang. It was his friend Jim. Jim was a brilliant, quiet researcher who loved to do adventurous things when he wasn't tracking a cure for neuromuscular diseases.

"Do you have plans for July Fourth weekend?" Jim inquired. Jim was such a good friend that Mitchell could admit that he had nowhere to go.

"No, I don't," Mitch answered candidly. "Why, do you?"

"As a matter of fact, I might. A few of my friends want to go to Lake George. They think that they can rent a small house there from Friday through Monday. If we can get five people who want to go, we can divide the expenses into a reasonable portion per person."

Getting five single yuppies on the Upper West Side to commit to anything was usually an ordeal. "Look," Mitch offered, "I don't want to do any organizing. If you can get all of the people together, find a house, rent a car, and buy food, I'll be happy to share the expenses. I'll even help prepare the food for most of the meals once we're there. Just don't ask me to make any plans or coordinate people."

"Great," Jim responded, very enthused. "I'll get back to you by the end of the week."

Tuning In

In typical Upper West Side style, Jim got final commitments from three others only five days in advance. Luckily for them, the house they wanted to rent was still available.

Mark, a tall, twenty-five-year old clothing salesman with dark curls, was going to buy all of the food they would need from a take-out store. Yoni, an Israeli, with Mediterranean features and a small build, had just passed his driver's test. He had recently bought a used car, and he was anxious to drive the entire five hours to Lake George all by himself. Jeff was a soft-spoken graduate engineering student with a trimmed beard and stocky build. While Jeff and Mitch had driver's licenses, their driving skills had atrophied after years of traveling only by subway in New York City. They gladly deferred to Yoni's desire to drive the entire distance. Jeff and Mitch offered to prepare and serve the meals.

The group planned to leave Friday morning bright and early, taking into account that it would be a long drive. Yoni showed up two hours late and Mark still hadn't bought a few necessities for the Sabbath meals. By the time the five troopers got on the road, it was 10:00 A.M. instead of 7:00. Mitch, the most orderly and punctual of the group, wasn't pleased that Yoni and Mark were so cavalier about making the rest of the group wait. They hadn't even had the courtesy to let the rest know that they were very delayed so that the others could spend their morning accordingly.

Half an hour into the drive the tension had subsided and everyone looked forward to a beautiful weekend. The weather forecast was for clear skies and temperatures in the low eighties from Friday until Monday morning. They couldn't have asked for better weather. The trip was uneventful, and the five travelers made pleasant conversation along the way. Mitch began to notice, though, that Yoni had a certain arrogance that rubbed him the wrong way. Yoni seemed sure about the correctness of every one of his opinions, and he had opinions about everything. He couldn't take suggestions from others or even hear that anyone else had a legitimate point of view that differed from his. Mitch tried not to let himself get too irritated, but he resolved not to spend much time with Yoni over the weekend.

By the time the young men arrived at their destination, it was not exactly what they had expected. The place was a bit rundown, the air conditioners didn't work, the kitchen did not have a functioning stove or oven, and the house had spartan furnishings. They spent the next few hours preparing simple meals for the Sabbath and arranging the accommodations as comfortably as they could. After dressing in clean clothes for the Sabbath, they kindled the Sabbath lights. They then chanted the evening services, let themselves be moved by the beauty of the surroundings, and sat down together for dinner.

By the next morning, the group members each did their own thing. Jeff went out for a sunrise stroll around the lake. Yoni and Mark slept late. Jim and Mitch discussed philosophy most of the afternoon. That evening, the mosquitoes outside feasted on anything that moved, so Mitch decided to turn in early. The others went out together to see what was happening in "town."

Sunday morning, Mitch wanted to swim, and then water-ski on the lake before it got overrun by tourists. The lake was lovely and inviting, and he made his way via a grassy footpath from the house to a remote spot. As he gingerly waded in, the shocking cold immediately numbed his skin and took his breath away. He decided to give himself five minutes to acclimate. When his teeth started chattering before his watch showed that the requisite time had elapsed, he decided that Lake George must be a location for catching frozen fish. Disappointed, he went back to the house.

Later, Jim and Mitch went hiking until it was time for dinner. When the group sat down to eat, they planned their schedule for the next day, July Fourth. Yoni and Mark had already investigated the fireworks schedules within a half-hour radius. Everyone was excited about watching fireworks at close range. New York City always had magnificent fireworks on the East River, but getting close enough to appreciate the spectacle meant fighting crowds of hundreds of thousands of people, or standing within deafening proximity of the

Tuning In

barges. Some in the group had done both, and they agreed that the fireworks had been truly awesome. Every time an explosion had occurred, they had felt the rumblings as the asphalt below trembled. Hundreds of thousands of spectators stood in a long, snaking stretch of the closed-off FDR Drive. They gaped and gawked as each colorful display was more spectacular in brilliance or configuration than the one before. The men agreed that they were glad they had done it once, but never had the desire to do it again. The thought of watching less impressive fireworks among only a few hundred, or at most, a few thousand people, was very appealing to everyone.

The only obstacle that the men anticipated was traffic. If they watched fireworks anywhere near Lake George, it meant not heading back to New York until close to 10:00 P.M. At that hour, they expected another five-hour return journey. Mitch had to work the next day, and three of the others doubted that Yoni should drive so many hours by himself at such a late hour. Yoni kept brushing off the criticisms, insisting that he usually kept late hours and that he would have no difficulty staying alert. The group voted four-to-one to watch the local fireworks before heading back to New York.

Monday afternoon, Mark and Mitch started packing up the car and prepared to close up the house after dinner. The group suggested that Yoni take a nap to make sure that he was well-rested when they set off that evening, but he assured them that it was unnecessary. He would be just fine.

At 8:00 P.M., everyone piled into the car and they drove to the park where spectators could watch the evening fireworks. Yoni insisted that he knew how to get there and proceeded to get hopelessly lost. This was before there were cell phones, and there were no gas stations or public phones in the area where the men could call someone to get their bearings.

Fifteen minutes after the fireworks began, Yoni finally pulled into the parking lot adjacent to the recreation area. It was now 9:30. The group watched a mere ten minutes of spectacle, then it was over. By the time they got back to Yoni's car, Mitch was dreading the long drive that lay ahead.

"Can you get us back onto I-87?" Jim asked Mitch.

Mitch reluctantly took two maps, studied them, and tried to get his bearings. "Yes," he replied, "it seems that we have to go back one-and-a-half miles on these local streets and then the main street here will intersect with I-87."

Meanwhile, a few hundred other people were also crawling out of the parking area and filing out onto the same streets that the men needed to travel. In triple the time that it should have taken had there been no traffic, they finally edged onto the cloverleaf that funneled traffic onto the interstate. Their view of the highway was initially shrouded by forest, but as soon as they nudged their way into the bumper-to-bumper traffic, they saw rows of red taillights as far as the eye could see. The cars barely crawled along, and the next exit was several miles away. At the rate they traveled, they would be on the interstate the entire night.

Jeff suggested, "Isn't there some alternate route that we can take back?"

None of the group was very familiar with upstate New York. For all they knew, they could have been in California. Three sets of eyes turned to Mitch. "Here, take this map. See if you can find another way to get back."

Mitch peered at the fine print on the map and it seemed to indicate that they could get onto Route 9 to take them back to New York City. "It looks like we can get off the next exit and get on an alternate highway just a few miles away," he recommended. "That highway appears to go back to the city, too."

Twenty minutes later, Yoni reached an exit and began traveling on a side road. It was pitch black, there were no road signs, and the hilly road continually weaved and curved. They had no idea where they were, and it didn't seem that they were likely to know much more until daybreak.

Tuning In

"If we continue on this road, the map says that we should reach Route 9, which will take us south to New York," Mitch advised. "If everyone agrees, we can stay on this for a few more minutes and see if we reach that highway. If a town appears, we can ask someone for directions."

The group decided to continue on the dark, winding road. Within minutes, Yoni had erroneously followed a left-hand curve that took them to a narrow local road. "Yoni," Jim insisted, "continue on this road until you can find a place to turn around, then make a U-turn and get back on the road that we just got off."

Yoni was visibly annoyed. "I know how to drive," he proclaimed, as the car went under a short tunnel and the road curved to the left. The car was plunged into absolute blackness as Yoni slowed the car to a stop. "Watch."

With that, he proceeded to put the car in reverse and tried to back the car through the tunnel that they had just exited. He planned to stay in reverse until he rejoined the highway that he had just turned off a quarter-of-a-mile before.

"Yoni," Mitch screamed, "make the car go forward! PUT IT IN FORWARD GEAR! You're going to get us killed!" In an instant, Jim, Mark and Jeff were all trying their best to cajole, convince and motivate Yoni to go forward. Yoni, for his part, was busy transforming stubborn arrogance into a flirtation with death.

"I know what I'm doing," Yoni assured only himself. "You'll see."

Yoni continued backing the car up. The rear of the car was about to enter the tunnel. Mitch saw a glimmer of headlights at the other end.

"GO FORWARD NOW, YONI, NOW! ANOTHER CAR IS COMING AT US!" Mitch screamed, hoping that his vehemence would overcome Yoni's self-righteousness. In a split second, Mitch saw headlights beaming from the center of the tunnel. He realized that due to the curve in the tunnel, the oncoming driver could not yet see them. Until he would hear the screeching of rubber as the other driver slammed on his brakes, the other car would be a missile traveling at fifty miles an hour into Mitch's side of the car. Worse, there was nowhere for another driver to maneuver. If he would veer in any direction to try to avoid Yoni's car, he would kill himself by smashing into the walls of the tunnel.

By that time, Yoni had stopped his car entirely. The five men were sitting ducks waiting for the other driver to plow into their gas tank. The other driver was within a few yards of Yoni's car when Mitch heard the scream of the other car's brakes. As the headlights came straight toward Mitch's line of vision, he prayed, "Please God, save us." Then he said the words that Jews have said for thousands of years in their final moments before death, "Hear, Jewish people, the Lord is our God, the Lord is One." He waited for his life review to pass in front of his eyes. The oncoming headlights were now ten feet from Mitch and hurtling forward. As he took what he thought was his last breath, Yoni's car jolted forward. Yoni had just managed to shift the stuck gear from reverse into forward. His car escaped a collision with the other car by a mere two inches. Yoni proceeded as if the entire incident had never occurred.

Yoni and his fellow travelers were extremely fortunate to be miraculously saved from what should have been a fatal car crash. Mitch had no doubt that the power of his prayers played a role in their being spared; still, one should not rely on miracles. It would be far better for drivers to realize that a car is a potent weapon that kills more innocent people every year than guns do.

Three days after this open miracle, Mitch went to synagogue to recite a special prayer of gratitude for being saved from a life-threatening situation, by the One Who is always watching. He realized, with frightening clarity, that he almost became a statistic – one of the forty-thousand Americans killed each year in car accidents. His voice choked with emotion as he felt a rush of gratitude to God for giving him more years to live.

A Leap of Faith

After many years of school and hard work, I decided to take a long-anticipated trip to New Zealand. My arrival at a youth hostel near Mount Cook coincided with the Jewish holiday of Hanukkah, an eight-day festival commemorating the moral and military victory of the ancient Jews over the Greek army in the second-century B.C.E.

The next morning, after a good night's rest, I began my exploration of the stunningly beautiful area. I asked a pair of young hikers who were staying at my hostel, a Canadian and an Israeli, if I could join them for a few hours when they trekked the trails of Mount Cook. They planned to spend that night in a mountain hut some eight miles away, then return the following day. I would accompany them for the first four hours, then turn around and hike back to my comfortable accommodations at the hostel.

Since they had many miles to cover, we started out at 8:30 after a hearty breakfast. It was cold and overcast, and we bundled up in our jackets and gloves. We trudged out of the hostel and marched at a steady pace a short distance along a hiking trail. It soon crossed a suspension footbridge that spanned a rapidly flowing glacial river, swollen by the melting snow.

As the trail meandered through fir trees, we traipsed along a mucky mess of mud and gravel. Half an hour later, we emerged above the tree line, and faced a huge expanse of rock-strewn glacier and exposed rubble. We stopped to gape at the mountain peaks towering above us, glistening with melted ice. We felt dwarfed by the awesomeness and grandeur of the scene. I was amazed at, and humbled by, the power

Tuning In

and strength of the Creator manifested by the forces of nature. Just then, a chilly wind rippled across the wilderness, and reminded me that nature's beauty was often accompanied by less-than-pleasant forces.

We continued on, noting the dainty faces of alpine flowers poking their yellow and pink petals above the rock-littered dirt. They were minuscule harbingers of the approaching spring and contrasted with the harshness of the lingering winter. We were enveloped in stunning silence, punctuated only by the echoing sounds of ice cracking high above us on the glacier, and the crunch of our hiking boots against the stones.

By 10:00, the clouds had parted, and the sun began to shine brightly. I opened my jacket in the much-appreciated warmth. We had now reached a crossroads. We would walk perpendicular to the mountain for a short while, and then ascend by a long series of switchbacks to an elevated trail that was blanketed by snow on either side.

The perpendicular walk traversed more rocky and muddy terrain, until we came to our first stream. The glacier that covered the mountain was melting in the spring air, and streams of frigid, grey water were rapidly cascading downhill until they reached the frothy, swollen river at the bottom.

As we surveyed the scene in front of us, we realized that there were no easy ways to traverse the water. We would have to find a large, stable boulder that the glacier had disgorged. It would give us a midway point to step on as we crossed to the other side. Cliff, the Canadian, ascended along the riverbank, and finally spied a rock face protruding from the foamy water that was clouded by glacial debris.

"We can cross here," he announced. "This boulder looks like it got lodged in between some other rocks, and it's about halfway across."

Shuki, the Israeli, reached Cliff before I did, and easily hopscotched across the water, using the boulder as an aid. Despite my years of dance training, I was doubtful that I could land squarely on top of the rock and not slide into the glacial flow.

Brushes with Mortality

Cliff leapt onto the rock and balanced there easily. "Jump across to the rock," he coaxed. From here, it's easy for you to jump to the other side." It was at least a six-foot span from the bank where I stood to the rock, and another six feet to the far side. Crossing the first part was harder than negotiating the second because the former was uphill. I had done stag leaps far longer than that in ballet class, but I had never landed on uneven, slippery surfaces. I visualized myself landing just next to Cliff and steadying myself. I took a running leap and my hiking boot landed perfectly next to his. There was no room to spare. From there, it was indeed easy to spring to the other side. Elated, we continued on our way.

Twenty minutes later, we encountered a second glacial stream that we needed to ford. This time it was Shuki who spied a rock poking through the surface of the roiling, dirty water. We descended some thirty feet along the bank of the fast-running river, and Cliff led the way across.

As we continued on our way, the strenuousness of the uphill climb, coupled with the now-mild weather, prompted me to remove my jacket and tie it around my waist. We had reached the switchbacks, and we snaked along the narrowing, rocky path, as the landscape became starker and more treacherous. Enough glacial ice had melted that the trail was quite muddy and slippery in places, and the drop along the side began to deepen. Even my hiking boots were no longer providing adequate traction for me to continue comfortably, so I announced to the men that I was turning back. Being men, they, of course, wanted to continue to their intended destination. I, being a woman, was concerned about my safety.

I asked if they would be so kind as to help me get back across the closest river, and they said no. They did not want to waste any time because they wanted to get to their destination by 4:00. Backtracking with me would add a half-hour to their trip and they weren't willing to do that.

I was stuck. I was in no way prepared to spend the night in a hut four hours further up the mountain, yet I was afraid that I would get

Tuning In

stranded if I returned the way I came. I didn't know what to do, but Shuki decided for me.

"Look, we're not waiting for you," he said. "I want to get to the mountain hut and we're not turning back."

Cliff looked helpless and reluctantly followed his partner up to the top of the switchbacks. I was left alone.

By now it was midday, perhaps 1:00 P.M. It was cool and sunny, but the weather in the mountains can be quite unpredictable. There could be a downpour at any time and it could suddenly turn freezing. What I didn't realize was that the beautiful weather would turn out to be my greatest enemy.

I slipped and slid my way down the somewhat obliterated trail until I reached level ground once more. I reckoned that it would be about another fifteen minutes until I encountered the river. Unfortunately, I also noted that it was sufficiently late in the day that no one else seemed to be traversing the trail that I was traveling. People had either started early in the morning, in efforts to reach the distant mountain hut, or they were enjoying short day hikes close to the hostel. Few people would be traveling anywhere near where I was.

I briefly entertained hope that I might get help when I noticed a Japanese hiker briskly walking several hundred feet behind me. He was quite nimble and seemed to be whistling a happy tune. As he got close enough to overtake me, I called out, "Can you please hike with me for a few minutes until we get to that river?" The river was now in sight.

He passed, completely oblivious to me or to my plight. It seemed, much to my chagrin, that he didn't understand a word of English. I kept calling out to him, hoping that my cries would signal him to at least slow down or investigate the source of my distress. Instead, he continued on his merry way.

A minute later, he reached the river. Without a moment's hesitation, as if he were a cartoon character, he simply bounded across without missing a beat. Before I could fix in my mind exactly where he had crossed the water, he vanished. There was not another soul in sight.

Brushes with Mortality

I continued hesitantly, feeling my anxiety mount as I neared the water. Even from a distance, I could see that the river was flowing much more powerfully than it had before. The warmth of the sun had melted the ice atop the mountain and the glacial runoff was forcefully pushing its way down to the river at the bottom of the mountain, carrying occasional rocks in its wake. The tributary in front of me was now wider than it had been when I had first crossed, and no large rocks were visible above the water's surface. What would I do? Pangs of panic began growing inside as I ascended and descended in a futile search to find a place to cross. It was clear that if I landed poorly while trying to get to the other side, I would quickly be washed downstream in a freezing slurry of rocks, gravel and melted ice. It was common knowledge among hikers that one could only survive for four minutes, at best, in these waters.

As I futilely waited for the water to subside, or for a fellow hiker to come to my aid, I remembered a story about a famous Hasidic rabbi who was imprisoned in one of the death camps during the Holocaust.

A Jewish apostate befriended him and they had many theological discussions during their forced incarceration. Meanwhile, they both became weakened and emaciated by the lack of food, the forced labor, the lack of sleep and the cold. One day, the Nazis ordered the inmates to go on a long march to an unnamed destination. When they were ordered to stop, the inmates were forced to stand at the edge of a huge pit that had been freshly dug. The Nazis' entertainment that evening was to tell the Jews that they had to jump across. If they did not reach the other side, they would fall into the pit and be shot. If they reached the other side, they would not be killed.

It was not humanly possible to span the width of the pit, so the apostate told the rabbi that he would simply jump in and get shot. The rabbi insisted that no matter how remote the chance, they had been given an opportunity to survive and they must avail themselves of it. The apostate was not convinced.

When it was the rabbi's turn to jump, he leapt across the pit and miraculously landed on the opposite side. As soon as the rabbi realized that he had survived this impossible test, he looked around and saw the apostate standing next to him.

"Rabbi," the apostate asked, "how in the world did you manage to jump across?"

The rabbi smiled. "I knew that I wasn't capable of jumping across that pit. So I closed my eyes and prayed that in the merit of my ancestors, the Almighty would save me. I then made the best effort that I could, and He carried me across."

The rabbi then posed the same question to the apostate. "But you, how did you get to this side?"

The apostate answered, "I held onto your coat."

I felt utterly helpless and decided it was time for me to pray. Perhaps I would also get Divine assistance. "Please God, help me get across this river," I cried out desperately. Then I took a running leap, closed my eyes, and hoped for the best. The next thing I knew, I was solidly planted on the far side of the torrent of water. To this day, I don't know how I got there.

Now that I had crossed this Rubicon, I still had one more obstacle to surmount. Since my prayers had worked so well the first time, I decided to try them once again. "Please God, help me get back safely to the hostel," I pleaded. In twenty minutes' time, I had reached the other angry swirl of water and debris, which was also swollen from the melting snow and ice.

By now, it was nearly 3:00. No one would be hiking up here any longer; it was simply too late in the day to begin a journey to this area. I surveyed upstream and downstream but could find no boulders peering above the water level. What would I do?

I have often read stories about people who face adversity and crisis with instinctive creativity and drive. I have never identified myself with those characters. My instinctive response to such crises is to freeze, and become immobilized. I did not have a wide gamut of similar experiences to draw upon, which would enlighten me as to how to traverse this seemingly impassable barrier.

Brushes with Mortality

Now that it was mid-afternoon, the air was becoming brisker as the sun began to descend from its zenith. My body was getting chilled from the perspiration that had evaporated along my back, and my shirt was damp. Not a soul was in sight, and I began to worry about the possibility of hypothermia if I got stranded for a long time. I looked up to heaven and implored, "Please get me out of this mess." I again scanned the river, searching up and down for a safe place to cross. My efforts were fruitless. I could not find a way to get to the other side.

Moments later, a group of ten mountain climbers appeared out of nowhere. They were coming from the direction that I had ascended hours earlier. What in the world were they doing hiking at such a late hour? They were armed with mountain-climbing gear, ropes, and special boots, and were heading toward the mountain hut where they intended to spend the night.

It seems that they had gotten delayed by a problem with their gear that had taken several hours to resolve. They would not normally have climbed at such a late hour, but under the circumstances, they decided not to cancel their trip. If they hurried, they would still make it safely to their destination before dark. How fortuitous for me! I called across the turbulent water and begged them to help me. They were only too happy to oblige.

The leader was roped in to another climber, and he leaped in his sturdy boots to a boulder that was under the surface of the water. His boots were waterproof and he was strong enough to withstand the pressure of the water current. I leaped toward him and he steadied me, and then helped me take a second leap to dry ground on the other shore. My feet didn't even get damp.

I thanked my helpers, who soon disappeared behind me. I stood quaking for a few moments from the realization of what could have happened to me. Whenever I would travel in beautiful and remote areas, some fellow traveler invariably recounted horror stories of what had befallen reckless hikers or climbers who had overestimated their abilities, or underestimated the challenges that lay ahead. I had always thought myself too conservative and too careful to fall into those same

Tuning In

traps. As I realized how vulnerable I had been exploring this vast and powerful wilderness, I felt in awe of the God that had both made it and sheltered me from its dangers. I felt like a tiny child enveloped in a protective Hand that shielded me from a potentially harsh and unforgiving world. I caught my breath as I realized my heart was pounding, less because of the exertion than because of my brush with my own mortality. After resting for a few minutes as I calmed myself down, I resolved never to be so cavalier again about my resourcefulness in the face of God's wonders. Realizing the message that I was meant to learn, I continued my trek back to the warmth of the hostel.

I learned a few obvious lessons that day, not the least of which was never to hike without a buddy, or without knowing what kinds of perils can await intruders to unfamiliar places. But the greatest lesson hit home when I lit my Hanukkah candles that night. The second blessing we recite after lighting the candles is that God "made miracles for our ancestors, during those days, at this time."

That day, I surely merited a miracle by holding onto the coat of my ancestors as I managed to get back safely to my base.

What You Don't Know Can Heal You

One December, I traveled to Montreal for a close friend's wedding. Much to my chagrin, upon arrival I discovered that I was unprepared for the bitter cold and unrelenting wind and their numbing effects on my sightseeing plans. The next morning, instead of seeing the beautiful Old City as I had planned, I decided to go to an underground shopping mall where I could purchase some warm winter boots.

As I stepped out of the house where a lovely family hosted me, I felt the wind lash across my face and legs as I ran toward a waiting taxi. I gave the driver the address of a store that my hostess had recommended and arrived at my destination some fifteen minutes later. I paid the driver, exited the cab, and tried to get my bearings. By the time I realized that I was in a totally residential neighborhood instead of anywhere near a shopping mall, the driver had sped away.

I was hopelessly lost. There were only attached houses sitting atop steps as far as the eye could see. There were no landmarks or recognizable buildings anywhere. I had no choice but to knock on someone's door and hope that they would be kind to a stranger.

I climbed the first set of stairs that I saw. As I reached the top, I breathed a sigh of relief when I saw a reassuringly familiar sight. A *mezuzah*, a parchment on which biblical verses are written, was affixed to the doorpost of the home. The Bible requires every Jewish home to

Tuning In

have a mezuzah on the doorway of every room (except for closets and bathrooms) and at the entrance to the house. Presumably, the owner was Jewish and might be willing to help a fellow Jew.

I rang the doorbell, not knowing what to expect. Living in New York, I was concerned that no one might be home this late in the morning. Or, worse, if someone were home, they would not want to open the door to a potentially problematic stranger. Initially, my fears turned out to be well-founded.

After what seemed like a long time, a woman's voice called from behind the door and asked me to identify myself. I sheepishly admitted that I was a lost American who was trying to find my way to a boot store. The voice replied that there were no stores in that neighborhood. She seemed to think that I might be using a ploy to gain entrance into her house.

I tried again. "I am a Jewish woman who came here for a friend's wedding. I was staying in Cote St. Luc and got bad directions to get to a store. I'm completely lost. Could you please tell me how I can get a cab back to the shopping area?" I pleaded.

There was silence. I tried once more. "Don't open the door for me. You don't know who I am. But could you please call a taxi to take me to the underground mall?"

Still, no answer. Soon, I heard the unmistakable sounds of someone releasing chains and unbolting locks, and the door slowly opened.

A short, sixtyish-year-old woman with reddish-brown hair swept up in a bun stood before me. She was at least a head shorter than me and matronly plump. She wore a shapeless black sleeveless dress with open-toed shoes. She sized me up very quickly and bid me to come in.

"My, my," she exclaimed, "it's freezing out there. Come in, come in." With a wave of her hand, she ushered me into her modest living room. As I started to rub my hands together in an effort to defrost, she kindly offered, "Can I get you a cup of hot tea?"

"No, thanks," I declined, feeling the circulation returning to my fingertips, "but thank you for letting me come in. I'm sure it must be a little worrisome having a stranger come to your door."

Brushes with Mortality

"Yes, it was," she admitted. "You see, I live alone. You looked innocent enough, though. What are you doing in this neighborhood? There is nothing here that would interest a tourist."

"I really don't know myself how I ended up here. A friend is getting married on Sunday and his friends, who are hosting me, told me that there was a great boot store in this area. By the way, where am I, and how far away is the address on this piece of paper?" I asked.

The lady studied the paper carefully, and then replied, "That's on the other side of town. It will take you half an hour to get there at this time of day."

"In that case, I guess that I'll just forget about shopping and get a cab back to the place where I'll be staying for the weekend. Can you help me to order a cab from here?"

"I'll be happy to," the lady replied, "only it will take a taxi about twenty minutes to get here. Make yourself comfortable in the meantime."

My first order of business was to take off my coat and enjoy the warmth emanating from the radiator. Meanwhile, as the woman leaned over the telephone book searching for a number, I got a better look at her. Her face was liberally wrinkled yet she beamed with a radiant smile. She looked like a grandmother who delighted in playing with her grandchildren. During the few minutes that it took her to get the telephone number and order me a taxi, I wondered why in the world I had ended up so far from my destination. I was not pleased about spending the rest of the weekend without a warm pair of boots. And I was very annoyed at having wasted the day going absolutely nowhere.

I was soon to find out that Someone had a more important plan for me than buying a pair of boots.

The woman hung up the receiver and walked back to where I was standing. She beckoned me to sit down, and seated herself on her faded green couch. She reassured me that the taxi would be here soon and graciously asked me where I was from.

"Well, I'm originally from Baltimore, but I've lived in New York for the past few years," I replied.

Tuning In

"Are you religious?" she inquired.

I wondered if there were something about my appearance that broadcast that I was. "Yes," I acknowledged, "but why do you ask?"

"If you're religious, and you're from Baltimore, then you'll appreciate the story that I'm going to tell you. I'm not religious, but my son is. He became religious when he was fifteen years old. Even though I wasn't interested in being observant, I was happy that he wanted that way of life. He asked to go to a religious school and decided that the best place for him would be at Ner Israel (a Jewish religious high school for boys) in Baltimore. So, I sent him there to study for the year.

"When he came home that summer, I was not feeling so well. Before he went back to school in the fall, he insisted that I see a doctor. I told him that I didn't think that I needed to, but I would go if that would make him happy. So, he came with me to see my doctor. The doctor did some tests on me and told me that everything was fine. He then told my son to go into his office and he spoke with my son for a few minutes. I didn't know it at the time, but he told my son that I had a tumor the size of a grapefruit in my stomach. My son was stunned, and didn't know what to say. The doctor told him that I couldn't be expected to live for more than three months, and that there was nothing medically that anyone could do to help me.

"My son didn't say a word to me about that conversation. He went back to school a few days later and told someone there what the doctor had told him. That friend told the head of the yeshiva. The head of the yeshiva announced that all of the boys and men in the school would pray for me at every prayer service, three times a day.

"My son came home for winter break a few months later and insisted that I see the doctor. I didn't know why he wanted me to go since I felt fine, but he wouldn't stop bothering me about it. I wanted him to be happy, so I finally went. The doctor did some tests and told me that I was fine. Then he called my son in the room with me and asked if I had done anything out of the ordinary since I saw him last. I said, 'No.'

Brushes with Mortality

"The doctor then explained that the grapefruit-sized, lethal tumor that he had seen about four months earlier had completely vanished without a trace. He had no explanation for how that could have occurred.

"My son did, and he told both of us what happened.

"That was eight years ago," the woman explained. "I've been in fine health ever since. I'm not a religious person, but isn't the power of prayer amazing? It saved my life."

Now I understood why I had ended up in this woman's living room instead of in a shoe store. I had prayed for so many things for years and it had seemed that many of my prayers had gone unanswered. I knew that prayer could change people's lives, but it had been a long time since I felt that that had happened for me. My prayers had become so lackluster that even though I prayed twice a day, I usually thought about a variety of other matters that had nothing to do with the prayers that I uttered. When I thanked God that my body functioned, I didn't feel grateful. While I asked the Almighty to give me health, or financial success, or wisdom, I might be focused on what I would eat for breakfast while I gave lip service to the words that I recited. As I requested that my Creator hear my prayers, I was often so distracted that I ruminated about what I would do at work that day. In short, I had stopped viewing prayer as something to take seriously.

This woman's son, and those who prayed for her in the yeshiva, truly believed in the power of prayer. They believed that if God created the world and runs it, He can surely, and often does, intervene in the lives of His creations. Prayer can create a spiritual conduit for overriding the laws of nature. We have to pray seriously, though, if we want prayer to be effective. If we pray with sincerity, there is no such thing as an unanswered prayer. We may not always get the answers that we want, but we will always be heard and be answered.

In recent years, there has been a spate of published research from reputable universities and medical facilities that have shown a remarkable phenomenon. This phenomenon has been replicated time and time again, even with ill people who are not religious. When

Tuning In

people pray for someone to get better, even when the sick person doesn't know that anyone is praying for them, the ill individuals get better significantly more often, leave the hospital sooner, and stay sicker less time than those for whom no one prays. The results have been replicated repeatedly with no scientific explanation for them. Religious people can, and do, have a way of understanding this.

That blustery day in Montreal a Divine Hand guided me to an unintended destination because there was a message that I needed to hear. It wasn't long afterward that I decided to co-author a book with Rabbi Yitzchok Kirzner, Z"l, *The Art of Jewish Prayer*. The encounter with this woman was a catalyst for me to realize that my prayers simply weren't what they could be.

I now know, with the passage of time, that many of my prayers weren't unanswered. I simply hadn't gotten the answers that I had wanted to hear at the time that I prayed. When we are equally ready to hear a "no" from our loving Heavenly Parent as a "yes" because we value the relationship and any communication that we receive, our prayers can take us to a different dimension. The prayers of the boys in the yeshiva undoubtedly took them to heaven. The woman I met was the beneficiary of prayers that brought heaven down to earth.